Angela Wade

BREAD
of
Heaven

Devotional Prayer Journal

Edited, Formatted, Designed & Published by

Wade Christian Publishing LLC

www.wadepublishers.com

info@wadepublishers.com

Bread of Heaven Devotional Prayer Journal

Second Edition

Written by Angela Wade

Paperback ISBN: 979-8-9864810-5-0

E-Book ISBN: 979-8-9864810-6-7

Dedication

I thank my husband, Dwayne, for your companionship and my children Donovan and David for your loving support!

Thank you to my parents, Deacon David & Deaconess Cheryl Williams, and Deacon Danny & Minister Marilyn Wade, for your faithful and dedicated examples of ministerial devotion!

I dedicate this book to all my mothers, Cheryl, Marilyn, Evelyn, Dorothy, Coleen, Rebecca, Amelia, Dianne, and late grandmothers Sadie & Idella that taught me the Word of God, taught me how to pray, ministers to me, and inspires me to remain steadfast in the Lord!

Thank you to all my family and friends for your prayers and support! I love you all!

Contents

Introduction

Bread of Heaven is literally food for your soul! This book was written to provide you with a weekly message and prayer to encourage, inspire, and uplift your Spirit. The Book of Genesis teaches us how to thrive and prosper against the spiritual warfare we are up against every day. God gives the Principles of Life in Genesis. Through Genesis, you receive a guide of life principles, instructions, teachings, lessons and examples to live by.

Open your mind, heart, and soul and receive the Spiritual nutrition that Bread of Heaven has to offer you! Allow your soul to get full and overflow with God's anointing and blessings over your life! My prayer is that this devotion will anoint your spirit, bless your soul, enrich your mind, and enhance your prayer life with God! May you receive wisdom and understanding of God's Word!

John 6:35 "And Jesus said to them, "I am the bread of life. He who comes to Me shall never hunger, and he who believes in Me shall never thirst."

Proverbs 3:13 "Blessed is the man who finds wisdom, the man who gains understanding"

Blessings,
Minister Angela Wade

Planting Seeds – Week 1

Genesis 1:11 - Then God said, Let the earth bring forth grass, the herb that yields seed, and the fruit tree that yields fruit according to its kind, whose seed is in itself, on the earth; and it was so.

Just as God planted seeds, you too must do the same, especially parents. You must plant the seeds of faith, love, knowledge and wisdom into your children. As a parent, you are your children's first teacher. Teach them the Word of God (seeds) and they will become God-fearing individuals. Educate your children with God's wisdom and knowledge. Teach by example how to apply Bible knowledge to life via everyday situations. The seed that you plant in them will grow and produce powerful anointed prayer warriors who will declare that Jesus is Lord!

Just as God saw that the plants were good, you too must see your children as good. You must declare and speak out loud in the atmosphere that your children are good because God said so! Use the power of your tongue that God has given you and speak positivity over the lives of your children (from as young as babies to even into their adulthood). Whether you are a parent or not, you should still sow seeds upon the children in your life. Just plant the seed and watch it grow!

Prayer: God, thank you very much for the seed! Thank you for teaching me how to plant seeds of wisdom and knowledge upon my children. Help me to give their seeds an abundance of love and nurture so that they will be a blessing upon others. I thank you for Jesus! You have taught me by example how to deal with life through your Son Jesus. Help me to continually teach and train my children so that they will always love and glorify You. In Jesus mighty name I pray, Amen!

Week 1 Devotion Questions:
- How often do you pray with your children?

- Do you read Bible stories with your children?

- How do you view your children in the eyes of God?

- Have you dedicated your children to the Lord?

Correlating Scripture:
- **Deuteronomy 6:1** - Now this is the commandment, and these are the statues and judgements which the Lord your God has commanded to teach you.

- **Deuteronomy 6:7** - You shall teach them diligently to your children, and shall talk to them when you sit in your house, when you walk by the way, when you lie down, and when you rise up.

Week 1 Bible Study:
- Read **Genesis 1** and **Deuteronomy 6**

- Teach your children the Ten Commandments **(Deuteronomy 5:1-22)**

- Teach your children the Lord's Prayer (**Matthew 6:5-13**)

Inspiration:

- Love your children the way that God loves you, unconditionally and wholeheartedly!

Devotion Notes

_____

_____

_____

_____

_____

_____

_____

_____

_____

_____

_____

_____

_____

_____

_____

_____

Faith From Within – Week 2

Genesis 1:12 - And the earth brought forth grass, and herb that yields seed according to its kind, and the tree that yields fruit, whose seed is in itself according to its kind. And God saw that it was good.

You have planted seeds of power and faith within yourself from God. You have to look within yourself and use your God-given power and declare victory against all battles. Spiritual warfare will battle you in various ways: your health, your relationships with loved ones, your finances, etc.

God has given you victorious weapons of faith, spirit and power. Use your faith to believe and know that God has already fought and won your battles on your behalf. Use your anointed spirit and speaking power to declare your victory and take back all the devil has taken from you and declare your riches, glory, and all forthcoming blessings from the Lord!

Prayer: God, thank you for your anointing! I thank you for your Holy Ghost power! You have embedded in me Your Holy Spirit so that I have the power to speak over my life and rebuke the enemy at all times! Thank you Lord! There is no other power as great as the Holy Spirit. With my tongue I can speak life or death because of You. You are majestic and sit upon the throne. I Love You Lord and will continually speak and sing praises from my tongue to You! In Jesus victorious name I pray, Amen!

Week 2 Devotion Questions:

- Do you have faith in God?

- Have you discovered and use your God-given power?

- What do you do when you're up against battles of life?

- How do you use your victorious weapons?

- Do you know that the battle is already won? By whom?

Correlating Scripture:

- **Mark 11:22** - So Jesus answered and said to them, "Have faith in God."

- **Romans 1:17** – For in it the righteousness of God is revealed from faith to faith; as it is written, "The just shall live by faith."

Week 2 Bible Study:

- Read **Mark 11** and **Romans 1**

Inspiration:

- Live by faith and declare victory in everything you do and over all situations you are confronted with!

Devotion Notes

_____

_____

_____

_____

_____

_____

_____

_____

_____

_____

_____

_____

_____

_____

_____

In His Image – Week 3

Genesis 1:26 - Then God said, "Let Us make man in Our image, according to Our likeness."

Genesis 1:27 - So God created man in His own image; in the image of God created him; male and female He created them.

God created all human beings in His own image. Regardless of your race, ethnicity, or gender, God created you to be distinctively like him! That's a special privilege and honor that you behold. Being created in God's very own image is the utmost distinction that anyone can uphold. You wear the image of God, the Father and King of heaven and earth! Let that thought sink in for a minute. So, both male and female are to live like the example that God exemplified through his only begotten Son, Jesus Christ. God gave Jesus to us to show us how to live our lives in the image of God.

Jesus was birth as a human on earth to experience life's trials and tribulations, sorrows and joys, and so much more. Jesus' life is the standard way of living! God shows you how to handle all situations that you may face on your life journey through Jesus. As a child of God, you have a duty to display God's image to all people at all times. When people see you, they shall also see the God in you too. You shall walk, talk, and live righteously so that your life glorifies God. By glorifying God with your life, you fulfill the image that God created for you. Therefore, always handle yourself accordingly unto God's Holy Will and Holy Word!

Prayer: God, thank you for Your Image! I wouldn't be the person that I am if it were not for you! Teach me how to fulfill Your Image accordingly. Help me to walk right, talk right, and do right. Allow my words and actions to always reflect your very own Image. I want to always honor You with my talents and gifts, help me to do so. God, you are Holy and deserve all the praise, glory, and honor! In Jesus Holy name I pray, Amen!

Week 3 Devotion Questions:
- Do you reflect the image of God? At all times?

- When and where do you express God's character?

- How do you handle life's trials and tribulations?

- In what ways does your life glorify God?

- How do you honor God with your anointed talents and gifts?

Correlating Scripture:
- **Job 33:4** - The Spirit of God has made me, And the breath of the Almighty gives me life.

- **2Corinthians 3:18** - But we all, with unveiled face, beholding as in a mirror the glory of the Lord, are being transformed into the same image from glory to glory, just as by the Spirit of the Lord.

Week 3 Bible Study:
- Read **Genesis 1, Job 33**, and **2Corinthians**

Inspiration:
- Reflect and display the image of God everywhere you go and with all whom you encounter every day.

Devotion Notes

_____

_____

_____

_____

_____

_____

_____

_____

_____

_____

_____

_____

_____

_____

_____

_____

Your Exceptional Gift From God – Week 4

Genesis 1:28 – Then God blessed them, and God said to them, "Be fruitful and multiply; fill the earth and subdue it;"

God has commanded you to be fruitful, multiply and replenish the earth with His children. Children are beautiful gifts from God. Children are in the significant stage of life where their hearts are pure and innocent just like Jesus'! Keep them pure by teaching them the Holy Word of God. Thank God daily for the children that he gives to you. You are to have children so that you can dedicate and give them back to the Lord to fulfill His Will here on earth.

God has a purpose and plan for your children. The children that you bear and birth will carry on your legacy and teachings. They will share the wisdom and knowledge that you instill into them and minister to others. Children are the exceptional blessing from God to you that will in return become a blessing to God, you, and others! They will glorify Him through their love for God and their works of helping others. God created people to form families that will honor Him and glorify His holy name!

Prayer: God, thank you for the priceless gift of my child/children! I thank you for their lives. Help me to nurture and care for them to the best of my ability. I ask that you show me to teach and train them the right way according to Your Holy Word! Allow them to always apply Biblical teachings to their lives every day. I dedicate my children to you and are extremely grateful for you blessing me with them. I Love You Lord! In Jesus wonderful name I pray, Amen!

Week 4 Devotion Questions:

- In what ways are you obedient to God?

- Do you know God's purpose for your life? Are you fulfilling it?

- How do you minster to the children in your life?

- When do you lead by example? Do you help and serve others?

Correlating Scripture:

- **Luke 18:16** – But Jesus called them to Him and said, "Let the little children come to Me, and do not forbid them; for of such is the kingdom of God."

- **Luke 18:17** – Assuredly, I say to you, whoever does not receive the kingdom of God as a little child will by no means enter it."

Week 4 Bible Study:

- Read **Matthew 19:13-30** and **Luke 18:15-17**

Inspiration:

- Make it a priority to be a blessing to someone else this week. Teach your children how to display God's righteousness.

Devotion Notes

_____

_____

_____

_____

_____

_____

_____

_____

_____

_____

_____

_____

_____

_____

_____

Nature's Best – Week 5

Genesis 1:29 - And God said, "See, I have given you every herb that yields seed which is on the face of all the earth, and every tree whose fruit yields seed; to you it shall be for food."

God has given you every seed-bearing plant and fruit tree for your food! God is the ultimate nutritionist! God has given you nutritious food from the soil of the ground to sustain you. He has given you every (not some but all) seed-bearing plants and fruits to eat thereof. Eating all fruits and vegetables as God commands will give you total health, wellness, and strength. Strive to eat nature's food just as God has instructed you. God has created you in His image and wants you to take care of the body that he has given you. Your body is the temple of Christ. Keep it clean with natural foods.

Prayer: God, thank you so much for the food of the earth. You have provided nutrition for me through your plants and fruits. Help me make healthy choices for my body. Allow my temple to receive all the vitamins and nutrients of the earth. Please remove all impurities from my body and restore me with total wellness. I thank You for your healing powers. In Jesus glorious name, I pray, Amen!

Week 5 Devotion Questions:

- Do you eat the natural foods God has gifted to you?

- How do you prioritize your health and wellness?

- In what ways do you take care of your body (God's temple)?

- Do you thank God for your health?

- When you're not feeling well, do you ask God for healing and restoration?

Correlating Scripture:

- **Leviticus 25:19** – Then the land will yield its fruit, and you will eat your fill, and dwell there in safety.

- **Isaiah 55:2** – Listen carefully to Me, and eat what is good, and let your soul delight itself in abundance.

- **3John 2** – Beloved, I pray you may prosper in all things and be in health, just as your soul prospers.

Week 5 Bible Study:

- Read **Genesis 1**, **Leviticus 25:8-22**, **Isaiah 55** and **3John**

Inspiration:

- Talk to God about your health. Give your cares to Him. Make your wellness a priority in your life!

- Eat healthy meals every day! Enjoy Nature's Best!

Devotion Notes

_____

_____

_____

_____

_____

_____

_____

_____

_____

_____

_____

_____

_____

_____

_____

_____

Very Good – Week 6

Genesis 1:31 – Then God saw everything that He had made, and indeed it was very good.

God proclaimed all that He had made (everything) and saw that it was very good! God has created and claimed you in His eyes as very good. You have to know and see the same for yourself. Know that you are good because (1) God created you in His image and (2) God has professed that you are. All people are good, some just don't behave as such because they don't know that they are. Acknowledge that you are good and then love and treat yourself as such! Treat others well too because all people were created very good.

Prayer: God, thank you for everything good! Help me to proclaim goodness over my life. Help me to see the good in others and allow others to see the good in me. I Love You Lord for you are good and mighty. You have omnipotent powers in Your Hands and controls all. I thank You for the powers you bestow upon me. Help me to always see and use my God-given powers for good. Lord, you are worthy of all praises. In Jesus marvelous name I pray, Amen!

Week 6 Devotion Questions:

- Do you view yourself as very good?

- How does it feel to know that God has already proclaimed you're good?

- How do you treat yourself and others?

- How do you use the powers God has bestowed upon you?

Correlating Scripture:

- **Romans 8:28** – And we know that all things work together for good to those who love God, to those who are the called according to His purpose.

Week 6 Bible Study:

- Read **Genesis 1** and **Romans 8**

Inspiration:

- God says you're very good! Have dignity! Treat others with respect and it will reciprocate.

Devotion Notes

_____

_____

_____

_____

_____

_____

_____

_____

_____

_____

_____

_____

_____

_____

_____

_____

_____

The Sabbath – Week 7

Genesis 2:2 - And on the seventh day God ended His work which He had done, and He rested on the seventh day from all His work which He had done.

Genesis 2:3 – Then God blessed the seventh day and sanctified it, because in it He rested from all His work which God has created and made.

The seventh day is declared as holy and has been blessed by God. The seventh day is God's blessing to you! You work and labor majority of the week. God has blessed you with a day that He has set aside only for you to worship Him and rest! How awesome is that?! Sunday is God's weekly refreshing gift to you! God has given you a day to replenish and rejuvenate your mind, body, and soul.

Read God's Holy Word, then pray and meditate afterwards to revive you mentally and spiritually. Sing His praises, revive your soul and give God all the glory, and honor that He truly deserves. You are to also gain physical rest for your body. Take the time on Sunday to allow your body to recover and recuperate from your labored days of the week. God gave you Sunday to give renew your mind, revive your soul, regenerate your Spirit, and restore your body with total wellness.

Prayer: God, thank you for the seventh day! Thank you for giving me the time that I need to recharge after my labored days. I am grateful for the revival that my soul gets and the rest that I receive every week. I cherish the time that I'm given to praise your Holy name! I am grateful for this day and will not ever take it for granted. God, you are wonderful! You are Holy! I worship you! I adore You! In Jesus righteous name I pray, Amen!

Week 7 Devotion Questions:

- Do you declare the Sabbath Day as Holy?

- Are you grateful for God's gift to you?

- How do you show gratitude unto God?

- Do you worship and rest on the Sabbath?

- In what ways do you revive yourself on the Sabbath Day?

Correlating Scripture:

- **Exodus 16:23** – Then he said to them, "This is what the Lord has said: 'Tomorrow is a Sabbath rest, a holy Sabbath to the Lord. Bake what you will bake today, and boil what you will boil; and lay up for yourselves all that remains, to be kept until morning."

- **Exodus 20:8** – "Remember the Sabbath day, to keep it holy."

- **Exodus 23:12** – Six days you shall do your work, and on the seventh day you shall rest, that your ox and your donkey may rest, and the son of your female servant and the stranger may be refreshed.

- **Matthew 6:6** – But when you pray, go into your room, and when you have shut your door, pray to the Father who is in the secret place; and your Father who sees in secret will reward you openly.

Week 7 Bible Study:
- Read **Genesis 2:1-7, Exodus 16, Exodus 20:1-17, Exodus 23:1-13**, and **Matthew 6:1-15**

Inspiration:
- Observe the Sabbath as a Holy day to worship God! Also take that day to truly revive yourself!

Devotion Notes

_____

_____

_____

_____

_____

_____

_____

_____

_____

_____

_____

_____

_____

_____

_____

Total Hydration – Week 8

Genesis 2:6 - But a mist went up from the earth and watered the whole face of the ground.

Before God created rain to water the earth, He used his majestic power and placed water upon the ground. Water was given unto all of the land! God has all powers in His hands! Water was given so that you may never thirst upon the land and to assist growth and nourishment of the plants and fruit trees that you are to eat thereof. Water is the best and purest substance that hydrates all of earth. Water has many important functions for you. It carries nutrients and oxygen to your body. It removes impurities from your body. It cleanses your body. It regulates your body temperature and so much more!

Prayer: God, thank you for water of the land! You are omnipotent and possess all powers of heaven and earth! You have given me a natural resource that is refreshing and soothing, just as You are! I thank you God for the cleansing properties that water beholds. You have given a substance that will keep me hydrated all of my days! I thank you for the enrichment of water! I give total praise unto You! In Jesus magnificent name I pray, Amen!

Week 8 Devotion Questions:

- Do you hydrate your body with enough water every day?

- What are the various ways you use water during the day?

- What steps do you take to conserve God's natural hydrating resource?

Correlating Scripture:

- **Isaiah 55:1** – "Everyone who thirsts, come to the waters;"

- **John 4:14** – But whoever drinks of the water that I shall give him will never thirst. But the water that I shall give him will become in him a fountain of water springing up into everlasting life.

- **John 7:37** – "If anyone thirsts, let him come to Me and drink. He who believes in his heart will flow rivers of living water."

Week 8 Bible Study:

- Read **Genesis 2** and **John 4:1-42**

Inspiration:

- God provides living waters for all whom believe in Him. Strive to drink a great amount of water every day!

Devotion Notes

Living Souls – Week 9

Genesis 2:7 And the Lord God formed man of the dust of the ground, and breathed into his nostrils the breath of life; and man became a living soul.

Who else in the Universe can form a man from the dust of the ground? Nobody but God! The only act that God did was to just simply breathe a breath. God's breath placed life into the soul of man! Man was lifeless until he received the "breath of God" that gave him a soul. This act alone displays that you are a spiritual soul in a physical body. Your soul is where your Spirit lives.

Your soul is the core of who you are as a person. Because your soul was created by God himself, you are and will forever be a child of God. Your physical body encases your soul so that everyone you meet or come upon can witness the Spirit and Love of God. God gave you the job to fulfill His Will here on Earth. God has a purpose and a plan for your life! Remain in prayer with God and ask Him to reveal His plan for your soul.

Prayer: God, thank you for the breath of life! Thank you for instilling your Holy Spirit into my soul! Teach me how to fulfill your Will. Teach me how to reveal your Spirit and Love to others. I thank you for the many blessings you have placed upon my life. I thank you in advance for all miraculous powers that you will bestow upon my life! I know you will fulfill my prayers in your timing. I ask that You Lord will continue to bless my soul so that I may bless the souls of others! You hold all powers in Your Hands!

Lord, I love and praise You! In Jesus miraculous name I pray, Amen!

Week 9 Devotion Questions:

- Do you know that God's Holy Spirit is in your soul?

- Do others experience God's love through you?

- Have you prayed for God to reveal His vision for your life to you?

Correlating Scripture:

- **Deuteronomy 6:5** – You shall love the Lord your God with all your heart, with all your soul, and with all your strength.

- **Isaiah 61:10** – I will greatly rejoice in the Lord, my soul shall be joyful in my God; for he has clothed me with the garments of salvation.

- **Matthew 22:37** – Jesus said to him, "You shall love the Lord your God with all your heart, with all your soul, and with all your mind."

- **1Thessalonians 5:23** – Now may the God of peace Himself sanctify you completely; and may your whole spirit, soul, and body be preserved blameless at the coming of our Lord Jesus Christ.

Week 9 Bible Study:

- Read **Deuteronomy 6, Isaiah 61, Matthew 22:34-40,** and **1Thessalonians**

Inspiration:

- Make it a priority to show God's love to others every day.

Devotion Notes

_____

_____

_____

_____

_____

_____

_____

_____

_____

_____

_____

_____

_____

_____

Tree of Life – Week 10

Genesis 2:8 – The Lord God planted a garden eastward in Eden, and there He put the man whom He had formed.

Genesis 2:9 - And out of the ground made the Lord God made every tree grow that is pleasant to the sight and good for food. The tree of life was also in the midst of the garden, and the tree of knowledge of good and evil.

God planted the Garden of Eden in the east. This is a great tip to acknowledge. Gardens receive the best sunlight from the east. As the sun rises each morning, vegetation receives God's great energy and keeps that energy as the sun moves overhead at noon. If you are to plant a garden, make sure it is located eastward. God gave you trees that are pleasing to the eye, the best gift ever! Take the time to get outside and enjoy the beauty that nature beholds. God also gave you trees that produce good food, which sustains your life.

God gives you natural vegetation to enjoy! Take joy in eating sweet nutritious fruits off of trees of life that God gave to you! God gave your soul discernment to know the difference between good and evil. You receive knowledge from God's Holy Word. Read your Bible to learn the knowledge that God want you to possess.

Prayer: God, thank you for the tree of life and knowledge! Thank you for the vegetation that you give to me! You give me healthy nutritious foods from the ground to eat thereof. Thank you for the serenity that nature beholds. Thank you for the sight of trees that gives tranquility and peace to my soul. Thank you for giving me the wisdom and knowledge to know the difference between good and evil. I pray that You Lord will daily uplift my soul with your greatness! In Jesus great name I pray, Amen!

Week 10 Devotion Questions:

- Do you sit and receive energy from God's sunlight every day?

- Do you take time to observe surrounding nature daily?

- Do you partake of God's vegetation?

Correlating Scripture:

- **Proverbs 2:10-11** – When wisdom enters your heart, and knowledge is pleasant to your soul, discretion will preserve you; understanding will keep you.

- **Ecclesiastes 2:26** - For God gives wisdom and knowledge and joy to a man who is good in His sight.

- **Isaiah 11:2** - The Spirit of the Lord shall rest upon Him, the Spirit of wisdom and understanding, the Spirit of counsel and might, the Spirit of knowledge and of the fear of the Lord.

- **John 1:4** – In Him was life, and the life was the light of men.

Week 10 Bible Study:
- Read **Genesis 2:8-25, Proverbs 1-4, Ecclesiastes 1-2, Isaiah 11-12**, and **John 1:1-16**

Inspiration:
- Take a walk every day and view the beauty that nature beholds. Connect spiritually with God outdoors. Let God breathe on you!

- Share God's wisdom and knowledge with others. Tell of God's greatness!

Devotion Notes

_____

_____

_____

_____

_____

_____

_____

_____

_____

_____

_____

_____

_____

_____

_____

_____

God's Placement – Week 11

Genesis 2:15 - Then the Lord God took the man and put him in the Garden of Eden to tend and keep it.

God will place you right where He wants you to be. Never doubt whether or not you are where you're supposed to be at in life. God has you where you are for a purpose and a reason. God gives you seasons within life and you are in the season that God designed for you to be right now at this appointed time. God wants you to work for and take care of the possessions that he gives you.

God will bless you with the desires of your heart. Those desires though also require work on your behalf. You are to labor to fulfil the blessings that God has in store for you. You are to also take care of all that God has blessed you with (your family, household, community, church, etc.) Once your blessings are fulfilled, do something kind and be a blessing to someone else.

Prayer: God, thank you for placing me where I am right now! You have placed me in this season of life for a particular reason. Help me to understand and know my purpose for this season. Help me to fulfil Your Will. Thank you for your overflow of blessings! Teach me how to serve others and be a blessing to others. I thank you for my placement in each season within my life! In Jesus sovereign name I pray, Amen!

Week 11 Devotion Questions:

- What season of life are you in?

- Have you asked God to reveal His vision for your life to you?

- Do you labor for God and bless others?

Correlating Scripture:

- **Numbers 12:6** – Then He said, "Hear now My words: If there is a prophet among you, I, the Lord, make Myself known to him in a vision; I speak to him in a dream."

- **Psalm 1:3** – He shall be like a tree, planted by the rivers of water, that brings forth its fruit in its season, whose leaf also shall not wither; and whatever he does shall prosper.

- **Ecclesiastes 3:1** – To everything there is a season, a time for every purpose under heaven.

Week 11 Bible Study:

- Read **Psalm 1**, and **Ecclesiastes 3:1-15**

Inspiration:

- Take good care of the people God gave to you (family, friends, church and community members).

- Strive to be a blessing to others. Every day speak a pleasant word to someone or perform an act of kindness.

Devotion Notes

Good Deeds – Week 12

Genesis 2:16 - And the Lord God commanded the man, saying, "Of every tree of the garden you may freely eat;"

Genesis 2:17 - "But of the tree of the knowledge of good and evil you shall not eat, for in the day that you eat of it you shall surely die."

God has advised Adam to eat freely of all trees except the Tree of Knowledge of Good and Evil. God is advising you also to stay away from evil matters. Evil surely comes with the death of your soul. When God created you, He declared that you are very good. Know and believe that you are good and do as such.

Speak good words and do good things. The soul of those that partake in evil will die. Strive to be the good person that God says you are. Live a good life, glorify God, and your soul will live forever. In death on earth, your physical body will return to earth and your soul will continue to live forever. Heaven will be the everlasting home of your soul.

Prayer: God, thank you for your counsel! Thank you Lord for your guidance every day! Help me to make the right decisions and to do the right things daily. Help me to speak good words and do good deeds. Guide my heart to do what is righteous. Use my tongue to speak the power of life over myself and others. Be a lamp upon my feet and the light upon my path. In Jesus righteous name I pray, Amen!

Week 12 Devotion Questions:

- Do you avoid evil matters? Seek for peace?

- What good deeds have you done?

- How do you glorify God?

Correlating Scripture:

- **Psalm 34:14** – Depart from evil and do good; seek peace and pursue it.

- **Psalm 143:10** – Teach me to do Your will, for You are my God; Your Spirit is good. Lead me in the land of uprightness.

- **Matthew 5:16** – Let your light so shine before men, that they may see your good works and glorify your Father in Heaven.

Week 12 Bible Study:

- Read **Psalm 34**, **Psalm 143**, and **Matthew 5:13-16**

Inspiration:

- Pray for God's guidance every day.

- Speak good words and do good deeds every day.

Devotion Notes

_____

_____

_____

_____

_____

_____

_____

_____

_____

_____

_____

_____

_____

_____

_____

_____

Help Mate – Week 13

Genesis 2:18 - And the Lord God said, "It is not good that the man should be alone; I will make him a helper comparable to him."

God, himself, spoke and declared that it is not good for man to be alone! God made the woman to be the helper of man. The man was created to labor and take care of his family. The woman was created to be man's helper and nurture the family. God even designed the bodies of men and women differently according to their godly roles. Because man is the laborer, his bodily stature is more muscular than a woman's. Man has masculine attributes to endure the labors of his work.

The body of a woman is designed with more fatty tissue so that she is able to carry babies in her womb, feed babies, and cradle babies all from her body. Woman has internal feminine attributes to endure the pain and sufferings of child labor, and to nurture her babies. Therefore, take pride in the gender God created you as and the roles that he has purposely designed just for you.

Prayer: God, thank you for creating me just as you have! You have created me for a specific purpose. Thank you for the intentional design of every part of me that makes me who I am. I will take pride and joy in the roles that I serve on your behalf Lord. You are awesome and majestic! In Jesus marvelous name I pray, Amen!

Week 13 Devotion Questions:

- Do you have pride and joy in the roles God designed for you?

- How do you labor for the Lord?

- Do you show your nurturing spirit upon others?

Correlating Scripture:

- **Psalm 139:14** – I will praise You, for I am fearfully and wonderfully made; marvelous are Your works, and that my soul knows very well.

- **Ephesians 2:22** – in whom you also are being built together for a dwelling place of God in the Spirit.

Week 13 Bible Study:

- Read **Psalm 139** and **Ephesians 2:19-22**

Inspiration:

- Perform a labor of love for others.

Devotion Notes

_____

_____

_____

_____

_____

_____

_____

_____

_____

_____

_____

_____

_____

_____

_____

Woman – Week 14

Genesis 2:22 – Then the rib which the Lord God had taken from man He made into a woman, and He brought her to the man.

God made a woman from the man's rib. God designed woman to have a womb that generates children for man. The location of the bone that God chose to create woman is very important. The rib is near the heart. When God gives a man a woman, He is giving man a precious gift that he is to hold near and dear to his own heart. The rib is also a strong bone that protects and encases vital body organs. Symbolically, man is also created to cover and protect his wife as well.

Prayer: God, thank you for the union of man and woman! Thank you for creating man to labor for, cover and protect the woman. Thank you for creating woman to love, nurture and assist the man. Thank you for helping me to fulfill the roles you have designed for me! In Jesus sovereign name I pray, Amen!

Week 14 Devotion Questions:

- Do you cherish the women in your life?

- How do you show appreciation to women?

- Do you hold God near and dear to your heart?

- If married or dating, do you dedicate your union/relationship to God?

Week 14 Bible Study:

- Read **Genesis 2:8-25**

Inspiration:

- Show appreciation to the women in your life.

Devotion Notes

Holy Matrimony – Week 15

Genesis 2:24 - Therefore a man shall leave his father and mother and be joined to his wife, and they shall become one flesh.

When a man unites with his wife under Holy matrimony, they both are in covenant with one another before God. The Holy matrimony is a promise to God that His glory will be displayed in your union. The woman and man vows to become one flesh under God. Holy matrimony is symbolic to Jesus Christ and his bridegroom, the church.

Jesus vows to love you unconditionally and to never leave or forsake you. Jesus is the way, truth and life. Jesus died for your salvation and is your ticket to Heaven. In your Holy matrimony, you are to remain one flesh until "death do you apart." And Jesus gave you salvation so that in your death, you will have everlasting life and meet your loved ones again in Heaven.

Prayer: God, thank you for the covenant of Holy matrimony! Thank you for your unconditional love! Thank you for salvation that I may enter Heaven upon my death on Earth. You are the way to the path that I will follow. You are the truth that my tongue will always speak upon. You are the life that has been given to me to glorify God with! Thank you God for all your wonderful blessings! In Jesus Holy name I pray, Amen!

Week 15 Devotion Questions:

- Is God displayed in your union?

- Are you evenly yoked as husband and wife?

- Are you aware that Jesus died for your salvation?

Correlating Scripture:

- **Ephesians 5:31** – "For this reason a man shall leave his father and mother and be joined to his wife, and the two shall become one flesh."

- **Ephesians 5:33** – Nevertheless let each one of you in particular so love his own wife as himself, and let the wife see that she respects her husband.

Week 15 Bible Study:

- Read **Genesis 2** and **Ephesians 5:22-33**

Inspiration:

- Show love to your spouse every day. Make a commitment to glorify God with your marriage.

Devotion Notes

_____

_____

_____

_____

_____

_____

_____

_____

_____

_____

_____

_____

_____

_____

_____

God's Guidance – Week 16

Genesis 3:3 - But of the fruit of the tree which is in the midst of the garden, God has said, "You shall not eat it, neither shall you touch it, lest you die."

You are to heed to the advice of the Lord. When you ask God for guidance, he will give an answer that you will hear on the inside of you. Know that God is trustworthy and will not steer you wrong. He is faithful and true. Following God's guidance will keep you from making unnecessary mistakes. Don't allow yourself to come across troubling experiences. Always ask God to give you guidance along the way and He will. And be sure to share your life lessons with others so that they too will avoid making gratuitous mistakes.

Prayer: God, thank you for your daily guidance! Thank you for being the lamp upon my feet that leads me each day! I pray that you continually guide my thoughts to help me make right decisions always. I pray that you guide my tongue so that I am to speak godly every day. Help me God to be bold in my good decisions and have control over any temptation that may come my way. Allow me to share life experiences and lessons with others. Teach me how to be a blessing and serve others. In Jesus mighty name I pray, Amen.

Week 16 Devotion Questions:

- Do you heed to the voice of God?

- When do you seek God for counsel?

- Are you mentoring or advising someone else?

Correlating Scripture:

- **Job 12:13** – "With Him are wisdom and strength, He has counsel and understanding."

- **Psalm 119:105** – Your word is a lamp to my feet and a light to my path.

- **Proverbs 1:5** – A wise man will hear and increase learning, and a man of understanding will attain wise counsel.

Week 16 Bible Study:

- Read **Genesis 3:1-7**, **Job 12:1-13**, **Psalm 119:105-112**, and **Proverbs 1:1-7**

Inspiration:

- Take the time to teach and share life lessons with others.

Devotion Notes

_____

_____

_____

_____

_____

_____

_____

_____

_____

_____

_____

_____

_____

_____

_____

Appearances – Week 17

Genesis 3:6 – So when the woman saw that the tree was good for food, that it was pleasant to the eyes, and a tree to be desirable to make one wise, she took of its fruit and ate. She also gave to her husband with her, and he ate.

Just because something looks pleasant, doesn't mean that it is good for you. The same concept also goes for people. Just because someone is beautiful on the outside doesn't mean that they are beautiful on the inside too. Don't judge a book by its cover only. You have to open that book, and look at its contents to make a sound judgment. You want to make sure that the people you encounter have pleasant hearts. You have to be careful about what you allow to enter your spirit. Keep your spirit clean and holy. Look beyond outer appearances and don't make foolish decisions.

Prayer: God, thank you for discernment! Help me to always see the good and bad appearances of things and people before I encounter them. Help me to comprehend so that I may make good decisions every day! Thank you for a sane mind that allows me to have logical reasoning. Thank you God for your wisdom and knowledge! Allow me to observe well and comprehend fully of all things. I thank You for loving and guiding me every day! Teach me to do what is in Your Will. In Jesus magnificent name I pray, Amen.

Week 17 Devotion Questions:

- Are you careful what enters your spirit? The people you keep in your company?

- Do you observe your surroundings carefully?

- Do you allow God to lead you every day? Ask for His daily guidance?

Correlating Scripture:

- **Psalm 25:5** – Lead me in Your truth and teach me. For You are the God of my salvation; on You I will wait all the day.

- **John 16:13** – However, when He, the Spirit of truth, has come, He will guide you into all truth; for He will not speak on His own authority, but whatever He hears He will speak; and He will tell you things to come.

- **2Timothy 1:7** – For God has not given us a spirit of fear, but of power and of love and of a sound mind.

- **2Timothy 2:22** – Flee also youthful lusts; but pursue righteousness, faith, love, peace with those who call on the Lord out of a pure heart.

Week 17 Bible Study:

- Read **Psalm 25, John 16:1-15, 2Timothy 1** and **2Timothy 2**

Inspiration:

- Keep a sound and righteous mind every day! Don't become fooled by worldly appearances.

Devotion Notes

_____

_____

_____

_____

_____

_____

_____

_____

_____

_____

_____

_____

_____

_____

_____

_____

Accountability – Week 18

Genesis 3:12 - Then the man said, "The woman whom You gave to be with me, she gave me of the tree, and I ate."

Here, Adam has placed the blame of his sin on Eve. Always take accountability for your own actions. Do not blame someone else for your mistakes. Take ownership of your faults and find ways to make them right. God is a forgiving God. He gives you grace and mercy. Grace is when God provides you with unworthy favor and love. Mercy is when God is compassionate and holds back deserved punishment. It's a blessing and a gift to receive God's unconditional love for you! God will not chastise you for your faults. Therefore, don't place blame on others. God has given you a conscious mind to know right from wrong and discernment to do what is right.

Prayer: God, thank you for your grace and mercy! Thank you for your unconditional love even when I don't deserve it! You continually give new blessings without judgments. Help me to always have a conscious mind to do what is right at all times. And if I do make any mistakes, help me to humble myself and ask of forgiveness from You and others. I love you Lord and give all praises unto You! In Jesus righteous name I pray, Amen!

Week 18 Devotion Questions:

- Are you accountable of your actions?

- Do you acknowledge your faults?

- Do you humble yourself and ask for forgiveness?

Correlating Scripture:

- **Exodus 33:19** – Then He said, "I will make all My goodness pass before you, and I will proclaim the name of the Lord before you. I will be gracious to whom I will be gracious, and I will have compassion on whom I will have compassion."

- **Ephesians 2:4** – But God, who is rich in mercy, because of His great love with which He loved us.

- **Ephesians 2:8** – For by grace you have been saved through faith, and that not of yourselves; it is the gift of God.

- **2John 1:3** – Grace, mercy, and peace will be with you from the God the Father and from the Lord Jesus Christ, the Son of the Father, in truth and love.

Week 18 Bible Study:

- Read **Genesis 3, Exodus 33:12-23, Ephesians 2**, and **2John**

Inspiration:

- Be responsible and mindful of all things that you do and say.

- Show unconditional love and kindness to others every day.

Devotion Notes

_____

_____

_____

_____

_____

_____

_____

_____

_____

_____

_____

_____

_____

_____

_____

_____

Activate Your Faith – Week 19

Genesis 3:14 - So the Lord God said unto the serpent: "Because you have done this, you are cursed more than all cattle, and more than every beast of the field; on your belly you shall go, and you shall eat dust all the days of your life."

Because the serpent brought sin upon the man and woman, God severely cursed the serpent. The serpent thinks he has powers over God's people but God demonstrated to the serpent that He has the majestic power! He declared that the serpent will forever crawl on his belly (face down to the ground!) Only God can declare such a force! The serpent will grovel in the dust as long as he lives. "Groveling in the dust" depicts uncleanliness. Don't allow the serpent to bring his filth into your life! Keep your Spirit clean with God's Holiness! Activate your faith and deter all filth!

Prayer: God, I come to you today asking that you continue to keep me in Your care! Help to keep all hurt, harm, and danger out of my life! Keep my heart and Spirit clean at all times! I deter and rebuke all the filth and wickedness that the devil possess. I will activate my faith and speak boldly and declare with my tongue that God is omnipotent and holds all powers upon His majestic Hands! God, You are righteous and Holy! In Jesus mighty name I pray, Amen!

Week 19 Devotion Questions:

- Who holds all majestic powers over your life?

- Have you activated your faith?

- How do you keep your spirit and heart clean?

- Do you rebuke away all evil forces?

Correlating Scripture:

- **Deuteronomy 7:9** – Therefore know that the Lord your God, He is God, the faithful God who keeps covenant and mercy for a thousand generations with those who love Him and keep His commandments.

- **Matthew 15:28** – Then Jesus answered and said to her, "O, woman, great is your faith! Let it be to you as you desire."

- **Romans 5:1-2** – Therefore, having been justified by faith, we have peace with God through our Lord Jesus Christ, through whom also we have access by faith into this grace in which we stand, and rejoice in hope of the glory of God.

- **James 2:26** – For as the body without the Spirit is dead, so faith without works is dead also.

Week 19 Bible Study:

- Read **Deuteronomy 6-8, Matthew 15:21-28, Romans 4-5**, and **James 2:14-26**

Inspiration:

- Proclaim your faith in God and do the works that God has assigned for you!

Devotion Notes

_____

_____

_____

_____

_____

_____

_____

_____

_____

_____

_____

_____

_____

_____

_____

_____

Spiritual Warfare – Week 20

Genesis 3:15 – "And I will put enmity between you and the woman, and between your seed and her seed; he shall bruise your head, and you shall bruise his heel."

This verse explains the Spiritual warfare that exists in this world every day. God has caused hostility between the serpent and the woman and hatred between the serpent's offspring and the woman's offspring. The hostility that exists is there as a constant reminder to the serpent that no matter what hatred he puts in the atmosphere or strife he embarks upon the woman; he will forever lose. You can expect troubles to arise but with God on your side, you will come out victorious each and every time!

Spiritual warfare will always exist but you must remember that it's not your battle to fight! Stay vigilant and remain faithful to God! Just stay prayed up and watch God fight for you! And because the hatred and hostility will exist generation after generation, you must teach your children God's Holy Word. Teach them how to pray and to develop their faith in God. Show them how to put on the full armor of God so that when they encounter evil, they know how to stand strong in the Lord. (**Ephesians 6:10-18**) God will allow the serpent to bruise your heel only. That means that God will allow to the serpent to strike you very little (not more than you can bear) for you to activate your faith and show the serpent that you are a victorious child of God. God has given you the power to bruise the serpent's head! God has already equipped you with powers (Holy Word, faith and prayer) to defeat evil! Rely on God and He will lead you to victory!

Prayer: God, thank you for your victorious powers! Thank you for the full armor! You give the belt of truth to rebuke evil and speak total victory. You give the breastplate of righteousness to do what is just. You give readiness that instills peace. You give the shield of faith to diminish all evil spirits. You give the helmet of salvation that I may have everlasting life in Heaven. You give the sword of the Spirit through Your Holy Word. I thank You Lord for your armor for no weapon against me shall prosper! In Jesus mighty and victorious name I pray, Amen.

Week 20 Devotion Questions:

- Are you aware of spiritual warfare?

- Do you speak and declare victory in the atmosphere?

- Are you faithful and give your battles to God?

- Do you teach and train your children how to pray?

- Do you use the tools of faith, prayer, and God's Holy Word to defeat evil?

- Do you wear the full armor of God?

Correlating Scripture:

- **Deuteronomy 20:4** – For the Lord your God is He who goes with you, to fight for you against your enemies, to save you.

- **Psalm 60:12** – Through God we will do valiantly, for it is He who shall tread down our enemies.

- **Isaiah 54:17** – No weapon formed against you shall prosper,

- **Romans 8:37** – Yet in all these things we are more than conquerors through Him who loved us.

- **1Corinthiansn15:57** – But thanks be to God, who gives us the victory through our Lord Jesus Christ.

- **Ephesians 6:11** – Put on the whole armor of God, that you may be able to stand against the wiles of the devil.

Week 20 Bible Study:
- Read **Deuteronomy 20:1-20**, **Psalm 60**, **Isaiah 54**, **Romans 8**, **1Corinthians 15:35-58** and **Ephesians 6**

Inspiration:
- Steadfast and stand firm in the victory of the Lord!

Devotion Notes

_____

_____

_____

_____

_____

_____

_____

_____

_____

_____

_____

_____

_____

_____

_____

_____

Strength and Endurance – Week 21

Genesis 3:16 - To the woman He said: "I will greatly multiply your sorrow and your conception; in pain you shall bring forth children; your desire shall be for your husband, and he shall rule over you."

Women experience intense pain and suffering during child birth due to the sin of Eve. Eve ate from the Tree of Knowledge of Good and Evil when God warned her not to. Even though childbirth is painful, holding your newborn baby is joyous. Life experiences are similar to that of childbirth. Suffering happens sometimes, but after the rain and storm comes the rainbow and sunshine. The rainbow to remind you of the bright and joyful aspects of life that are great (the rainbow is God's Covenant that He will never flood the earth again) and the sunshine to give you God's energy and strength to endure what's yet ahead of you.

God also declares that the woman's desire shall be to her husband and that he shall rule over her. Understand that God gives authority to devoted men that seek Him and are after His own heart. A man after God's heart is loving (**Psalm 18:1**), reverent (**Psalm 18:3**), faithful (**Psalm 23:6**), trusting (**Psalm 27:1**), respectful (**Psalm 31:9**), and obedient to God (**Psalm 119:34**). A godly man that loves the Lord will take great pride in leading his wife in a righteous way and she will gladly follow. The husband will be able to lead his wife by the examples and teachings of Christ.

Prayer: God, thank you for the strength that you give to endure the storms and sufferings of life! Thank you for your unconditional love. There is none like You Lord! God, I place my trust in You and seek your face! You are the God of my salvation! I give you total praise and worship! Place Your Holy Spirit upon me Lord! Teach me Your Holy Word that I may live righteously in all thy ways. I love You Lord! In Jesus Holy name I pray, Amen!

Week 21 Devotion Questions:

- Have you ever done something God told you not to do? What happened?

- Did your suffering bring forth future obedience to God?

- Do you live and lead by the examples and teachings of Jesus Christ?

- Do you live righteously in all thy ways?

Correlating Scripture:

- **Exodus 15:2** – The Lord is my strength and song, and he has become my salvation; He is my God, and I will praise Him.

- **1Chronicles 16:11** – Seek the Lord and His strength; seek His face evermore!

- **Psalm 28:7** – The Lord is my strength and my shield; my heart trusted in Him, and I am helped; therefore my heart greatly rejoices, and with my song I will praise Him.

- **Philippians 4:13** – I can do all things through Christ who strengthens me.

Week 21 Bible Study:

- Read **Exodus 15, 1Chronicles 16, Psalm 28**, and **Philippians 4**

Inspiration:

- Accomplish all your goals with God's strength and endurance.

Devotion Notes

_____

_____

_____

_____

_____

_____

_____

_____

_____

_____

_____

_____

_____

_____

_____

_____

_____

_____

Man's Labor – Week 22

Genesis 3:17 – Then to Adam He said, "Because you have heeded the voice of your wife, and have eaten from the tree of which I commanded you, saying, "You shall not eat of it." "Cursed is the ground for your sake; in toil you shall eat of it all the days of your life."

God is telling man that his work will not be easy on Earth. His labor will bring struggles and will take a strenuous effort to accomplish tasks. In order for man to live and survive, he will have to work hard to make his living. Even though man's labor is tough, God gives him the strength and endurance to do so. To endure the labor, man need a relationship with God to give him the ability to handle it all. Even when struggles arise, God still doesn't put more on you than you can bear. Life is a test of trials and tribulations that creates a testimony proclaiming God's glory and greatness!

Prayer: God, thank you for the labor and struggles of life that shows me my own strength. The tests and trials that I go through encourages me to rely on my faith and boldly proclaim that you are God Almighty who can do all things! God, thank you for continually covering me and blessing me. Lord, you are my shepherd and I shall not want. There's none like you Lord! In Jesus mighty name I pray, Amen!

Week 22 Devotion Questions:
- How do you labor for the Lord?

- Are you thankful for and appreciate man's labor?

- Do you show love to the men in your life? In what ways?

- Do you have a relationship with God? What is it like?

- How has God blessed you? What testimonies do you have to tell?

- Do you rely on your faith when struggles arise?

Correlating Scripture:
- **Deuteronomy 2:7** – "For the Lord your God has blessed you in all the work of your hand. He knows your trudging through this great wilderness. These forty years the Lord your God has been with you; you have lacked nothing.

- **Deuteronomy 5:13** – Six days you shall labor and do all your work.

- **Psalm 23:1** – The Lord is my shepherd; I shall not want.

- **Psalm 128:2** – When you eat the labor of your hands, you shall be happy, and it shall be well with you.

- **Psalm 128:4** – Behold, thus shall the man be blessed who fears the Lord.

Week 22 Bible Study:

- Read **Deuteronomy 2:1-7**, **Deuteronomy 5**, **Psalm 23**, and **Psalm 128**

Inspiration:

- Thank God for the job that provides you income! As God bless you, be a blessing to someone else.

Devotion Notes

_____

_____

_____

_____

_____

_____

_____

_____

_____

_____

_____

_____

_____

_____

Mother – Week 23

Genesis 3:20 - And Adam called his wife's name Eve, because she was the mother of all living.

Eve is the mother of all living. Women are titled mothers because they are the origin of life. Their bodies inhabit the development and growth of newborn babies and then prepare to give birth which initiates the beginning of life on Earth for children. A mother's role is to love and nurture her children. The task of a mother is loving and challenging. She must raise her children up to live righteously and just. Mothers, please teach your children to love God and always put Him first in their lives.

Motherhood is a selfless and tiring job but rewarding above all difficulties. **Proverbs 22:6** says "Train up a child in the way he should go: and when he is old, he will not depart from it." Mothers teach and instill the Word of God in your children. Mothers have the unique role of equipping children with God's love and teach them how to discover their purpose in life. Teach children how to pray and cast their cares upon the Lord. Direct children in the right path and they will learn how to use their gifts and talents for God as adults.

Prayer: God, thank you for all mothers! Asking God to give mothers the wisdom they need to teach their children how to live righteously. Give mothers the strength and guidance they need daily to take care of their children. Allow the love that mothers pour into their children return back to them abundantly. Teach children how to rely on You God and show love and kindness to others. Thank you God for the wonderful blessing of motherhood all over this world! We thank you Lord for your glory! In Jesus wonderful name we pray, Amen!

Week 23 Devotion Questions:

- How do you show love to the mothers in your life?

- Do you love God and put Him first in your life?

- Do you help children discover their purpose in life?

- What anointed talents and gifts has God blessed you with?

Correlating Scripture:

- **Deuteronomy 5:16** – Honor your father and mother, as the Lord your God has commanded you, that your days may be long, and that it may be well with you in the land which the Lord your God is giving you.

- **Proverbs 23:25** – Let your father and your mother be glad, and let her who bore you rejoice.

- **Proverbs 31:28** – Her children rise up and call her blessed.

- **Colossians 3:20** – Children, obey your parents in all things, for this is well pleasing to the Lord.

Week 23 Bible Study:

- Read **Genesis 3**, **Proverbs 23:15-25**, **Proverbs 31**, and **Colossians 3:18-25**

Inspiration:

- Do something special for your mother, or in remembrance of her.

Devotion Notes

_____

_____

_____

_____

_____

_____

_____

_____

_____

_____

_____

_____

_____

_____

_____

_____

Righteous and Just – Week 24

Genesis 4:7 – If you do well, will you not be accepted? And if you do not well, sin lies at the door. And its desire is for you, but you should rule over it.

Always strive to do what's right upon the Lord. If you chose to do the wrong things, then sin will be waiting to control you. It's easier and takes less effort to do what's right than to make a deliberate effort to do what's wrong. Strive every day to do good deeds and speak good words. Put goodness into the atmosphere so that it will always be upon you. Always do what's right in the sight of God. God has already equipped you with the power of the tongue to speak life and rebuke sin. Plead upon the blood of Jesus and do so with authority and power. Let the devil know that he does not have any control over you or your life. With God, you must subdue sinful temptations and be strong within your Spirit and always do right!

Prayer: God, thank you for a strong mind and a loving heart. Continue to help me always do what is right in thy sight. Always allow me to speak the tongue of life over death. Give me daily strength and power to rebuke the devil and all his evil ways. Allow my life to shine the light of the Lord everywhere I go and in all things that I do! God, you are Holy and are worthy of all my praises! Keep me in Your loving care and protection! In Jesus sovereign name I pray, Amen!

Week 24 Devotion Questions:

- Do you strive daily to do what's right?

- Do you speak good words? Have good deeds?

- How do you put righteousness into the atmosphere?

- Who has control over your life?

Correlating Scripture:

- **Psalm 18:20** – The Lord rewarded me according to my righteousness; according to the cleanness of my hands he has recompensed me.

- **Micah 6:8** – He has shown you, O man, what is good; and what does the Lord require of you but to do justly, to love mercy, and to walk humbly with your God?

- **Matthew 6:33** – But seek first the kingdom of God and His righteousness, and all these things shall be added to you.

- **Ephesians 4:24** – And that you put on the new man which was created according to God, in true righteousness and holiness.

Week 24 Bible Study:

- Read **Genesis 4, Psalm 18, Micah 6, Matthew 6**, and **Ephesians 4-5**

Inspiration:

- Make deliberate efforts to do the right things at all times.

Devotion Notes

Sweet Jesus – Week 25

Genesis 4:26 – And as for Seth, to him also a son was born; and he named him Enosh. Then men began to call on the name of the Lord.

This is the time in the Bible where first generations of people began to call upon the name of the Lord. People began worshipping the Lord and calling upon His name. You can call on the name of Jesus at any hour of any day! He hears your cry and God hears your prayers! Songwriter Bishop Rance Allen wrote in his song that "There's something about the name Jesus! It is the sweetest name I know." There is no name sweeter than that of Jesus Christ, our Lord and Savior who died upon the cross for the salvation of us all! The name Jesus alone has power that no other has!

Prayer: God, thank you for only begotten son, Jesus Christ! You gave me a Savior that died and paid the price for my sins and inequities. And with the faith of a mustard seed and the confessions of my tongue, I can repent and receive Salvation and have everlasting life with You Lord! Thank you for my life! Help me to fulfill the purpose you have for me and allow me to do Your Will. Help me be a blessing and a service unto others. In Jesus magnificent name I pray, Amen!

Week 25 Devotion Questions:

- Do you call upon the name of the Lord?

- Do you worship God? In what ways?

- Do you have faith and receive Christ's Salvation?

- Have you acknowledged God's calling on your life?

Correlating Scripture:

- **John 3:16** – For God so loved the world that He gave His only begotten Son, that whoever believes in Him should not perish but have everlasting life.

- **Galatians 3:26** – For you are all sons of God though faith in Christ Jesus.

- **Galatians 6:18** – Brethren, the grace of our Lord Jesus Christ be with your spirit. Amen.

- **Colossians 3:17** – And whatever you do in word or deed, do all in the name of the Lord Jesus, giving thanks to God the Father through Him.

Week 25 Bible Study:

- Read **John 3**, **Galatians 3:19-29**, **Galatians 6**, and **Colossians3**

Inspiration:

- Call out on the name of Jesus and cast your cares upon Him!

Devotion Notes

_____

_____

_____

_____

_____

_____

_____

_____

_____

_____

_____

_____

_____

_____

_____

Creation – Week 26

Genesis 5:1 – In the day that God created man, He made him in the likeness of God.

Genesis 5:2 – He created them male and female, and blessed them, and called them Mankind in the day they were created.

God created all people in His image. Humans were created to be like God, to display His greatness! All men, women, boys and girls are blessed by God. Take pride in the fact that when someone sees you, they shall also see the presence of God within you! God is great! God is good! God is love! God is patient! God is kind! God is majestic! God is wonderful! God is joy! God is peace! Be sure to uphold God's many characteristics! Carry the honor of His image with you everywhere you go! Let God's light shine bright within you!

Prayer: God, thank you for creating me in Your image! To be like You is an honor that I will uphold every day of my life! Thank you for your blessing of creation! Thank you for my life and the lives of my family and friends! We are nothing without You Lord. Allow our lives to be fulfilled with the works of Your Will. Help us to live like You and inspire others to do so too! God, we give You all the glory, honor and praise! In Jesus Holy name we pray, Amen!

Week 26 Devotion Questions:

- Do you thank God for His creation? You?

- Do you reflect the image of God? His characteristics?

- How do you display God's greatness?

Correlating Scripture:

- **Galatians 5:22** – But the fruit of the Spirit is love, joy, peace, longsuffering, kindness, goodness, faithfulness, gentleness, self-control.

- **1John 4:4** – You are of God, little children, and have overcome them, because He who is in you is greater than he who is in the world.

Week 26 Bible Study:

- Read **Genesis 5**, **Galatians 5**, and **1John 4**

Inspiration:

- Make sure that God's image and light are shining through you daily.

Devotion Notes

_____

_____

_____

_____

_____

_____

_____

_____

_____

_____

_____

_____

_____

_____

Born Warriors – Week 27

Genesis 6:4 – There were giants on the earth in those days, and also afterward, when the sons of God came in to the daughters of men and they bore children to them. Those were the mighty men who were of old, men of renown.

This scripture tells of when the sons of God had intercourse with women, the children born became the heroes and famous warriors of those ancient times. This still holds truth even today! Children of God give birth to Warriors of the next generation. In today's evil and wicked world, God is birthing children that will overcome with His wisdom and power! Each generation of children are born wiser and smarter! They are born warriors that's equipped for the spiritual warfare that exists.

God has prepared His Warriors to receive the victory of all battles! Parents, teach your children the Word of God so that they know the truth according to His Holy Word! Teach children how to pray and they will always stand firm and rebuke anything that is not of the Lord.

Prayer: God, thank you for your Born Warriors! Thank you for the children that you gift to us! Allow all children of each generation to be a blessing to others. Teach them how to use their God given power of prayer to condemn evil forces that they may come up against. Help them to see the Warrior in themselves and speak boldly and with authority that God is Lord of all! Let them always and forever stand firm on Your Holy Word! In Jesus name I pray, Amen!

Week 27 Devotion Questions:

- Are you a born warrior? Do you see the Warrior in yourself? In your children?

- Have you thanked God for blessing you with the children in your life?

- Do you use your power of prayer to defeat the enemy?

Correlating Scripture:

- **Proverbs 22:6** – Train up a child in the way he should go, and when he is old he will not depart from it.

- **Ephesians 6:4** – And you, fathers, do not provoke your children to wrath, but bring them up in the training and admonition of the Lord.

- **Ephesians 6:19** – And for me, that utterance may be given to me, that I may open my mouth boldly to make known the mystery of the gospel.

Week 27 Bible Study:

- Read **Genesis 6**, **Proverbs 22**, and **Ephesians 6**

Inspiration:

- Boldly speak triumph everywhere you go!

Devotion Notes

Favor of the Lord – Week 28

Genesis 6:8 - But Noah found grace in the eyes of the Lord.

You must be like Noah and find favor with the Lord. You can find the Lord's favor by having the love of God in your heart. When you love God, He allows agape love to be poured from your heart upon others. Strive to always speak kind words to others and do nice deeds for others.

In **Matthew 22: 37-39** Jesus states, "Love the Lord your God with all your heart and with all your soul and with all your mind: Love your neighbor as yourself." Basically, love God and do unto others as you would have them do unto you and you will find favor with the Lord!

Prayer: God, thank you for favor, grace and mercy! Thank you for Your acceptance and approval of my soul! Thank you for giving me what I don't deserve! Thank you for protecting me from the punishments that I do deserve! Thank you for your many blessings Lord! Help me to use my blessings to be a blessing unto someone else. I love you God with all my heart, mind, and soul! In Jesus magnificent name I pray, Amen!

Week 28 Devotion Questions:

- Have you inherited the love of God in your heart?

- How do you show agape love to others? In what ways?

- Do you treat others the way you would like to be treated?

- Do you think God is happy with your use of His Holy Spirit?

Correlating Scripture:

- **Leviticus 19:18** – You shall not take vengeance, nor bear any grudge against the children of your people, but you shall love your neighbor as yourself: I am the Lord.

- **Matthew 7:12** – Therefore, whatever you want men to do to you, do also to them, for this is the Law and the Prophets.

- **1John 4:7** – Beloved, let us love one another, for love is of God; and everyone who loves is born of God and knows God.

Week 28 Bible Study:

- Read **Leviticus 19**, **Matthew 7**, and **1John 4:7-19**

Inspiration:

- Make a conscious choice to love and serve others always!

Devotion Notes

_____

_____

_____

_____

_____

_____

_____

_____

_____

_____

_____

_____

_____

_____

_____

_____

Fellowship with God – Week 29

Genesis 6:9 - Noah was a just man, perfect in his generations. Noah walked with God.

God shows the example of righteousness through Noah. You are to love God and trust His Word just as Noah did. Noah believed God's promises and kept his faith in Him. God wants to be in close fellowship with you as well. Allow yourself to fellowship with God; and when you do, He will place serenity over your life! God is the only one who can give you peace and calm like no other. God's tranquility is the best gift in life you can ever receive!

Prayer: God, thank you for Your fellowship! You give love and peace like none other! You bring calmness to my mind and peace to my soul! God, help me to walk daily with You. Guide my footsteps Lord. Keep me on a righteous path. You are my wonderful counselor and I thank you God for your guidance day to day. I worship your Holy name Lord! In Jesus sovereign name I pray, Amen!

Week 29 Devotion Questions:

- Do you love God with your whole heart?

- Do you trust God's Holy Word?

- How do you fellowship with God?

- Do you still worry after praying?

Correlating Scripture:

- **1John 1:3** – That which we have seen and heard we declare to you, that you also may have fellowship with us; and truly our fellowship is with the Father and with His Son Jesus Christ.

- **1Corinthians 1:9** – God is faithful, by whom you were called into the fellowship of His Son, Jesus Christ our Lord.

- **2Corinthians 13:14** – The grace of the Lord Jesus Christ, and the love of God, and the communion of the Holy Spirit be with you all. Amen.

Week 29 Bible Study:

- Read **1John 1**, **1Corinthians 1**, and **2Corinthians 13**

Inspiration:

- Pray in fellowship with God! When you pray, really give all your burdens to God and worry about nothing! Pray about everything, free your mind and receive God's serene peace!

Devotion Notes

God's Covenant – Week 30

Genesis 6:18 - But I will establish My covenant you; and you shall shalt go into the ark – you, your sons, your wife, and your sons' wives with you.

Genesis 6:22 - Thus Noah did; according to all that God commanded him, so he did.

God has established His covenant with you! You just have to heed to His voice and fulfill His Will for your life! God has promised to always be with you and never leave you! God has given you many promises and blessings along life's journey. Stand firm and hold on to God's unchanging hand as He deliver His promises to you! God is a man that keeps His Word unto you. He will never leave you or forsake you. You can place all your faith and trust in the Lord and know that He will deliver to you what you pray for.

You have to be just like Noah. God told Noah that He will confirm His covenant with him. Noah then placed his trust in God and did what God asked of him even before he knew what was yet to come. You too have to trust God even before receiving your blessing. When God said "But I will confirm my covenant with you", was an indication that Noah hadn't received the blessing yet. But Noah displayed his faith and did the work that God commanded him to do. Noah knew that God was going to keep His promises to him. Noah also knew that God was about to bless him and his family because God told him that He was going to confirm the covenant. You too have to keep your faith and place your trust in God and believe that He will bless you too!

Prayer: God, thank you for your covenant! Thank you for blessing me abundantly! Help me to always keep my faith and trust in you, Lord! Guide me and direct my works for You! Allow me to fulfill Your Will for my life! Allow my blessings to be blessings upon others! Thank you God for keeping Your promises and for never leaving my side! I give all glory, honor and praises unto You! In Jesus victorious name I pray, Amen!

Week 30 Devotion Questions:

- Are you in covenant with God?

- Do you sincerely place all your faith and trust in God?

- Do you hear God's voice? Do you obey God when He speaks to you?

- Are you doing the ministry works that God has commanded you to do?

- Do you believe God's promises to you?

Correlating Scripture:

- **Exodus 34:10** – And He said: "Behold, I make a covenant. Before all your people I will do marvels such as have not been done in all the earth, not in any nation; and all the people among whom you are shall see the work of the Lord. For it is an awesome thing that I will do with you."

- **Leviticus 26:9** – "For I will look on you favorably and make you fruitful, multiply you and confirm My covenant with you."

- **2 Samuel 7:28** – "And now, O Lord God, You are God, and Your words are true, and You have promised this goodness to Your servant."
- **1Chronicles 17:20** – O Lord, there is none like You, nor is there any God besides You, according to all that we have heard with our ears.

- **Nehemiah 1:5** – And I said: "I pray, Lord God of Heaven, O great and awesome God, You who keep Your covenant and mercy with those who love You and observe Your commandments."

Week 30 Bible Study:
- Read **Genesis 6, Exodus 34, Leviticus 26, 2Samuel 7, 1Chronicles 16 - 17**, and **Nehemiah 1**

Inspiration:
- Trust and praise God even before receiving the blessing!

Devotion Notes

_____

_____

_____

_____

_____

_____

_____

_____

_____

_____

_____

_____

_____

_____

_____

_____

Clean Foods – Week 31

Genesis 7:2 - You shall take with you seven each of every clean animal, a male and his female.

Genesis 9:3 - Every moving thing that lives shall be food for you. I have given you all things, even as the green herbs.

God has given the food guide for eating. God told Noah to take the clean beasts that he has approved for eating and for sacrifice. In **Leviticus 11:3**, God has given instruction to only eat clean animals that has a combination of split hooves and chews the cud, such as cattle, deer, sheep and goats.   In **Leviticus 11:9**, God also gives permission to eat the marine animals that only has fins and scales. God also has given green herbs to eat thereof. In your diet, try to consume only the clean animals God commands. Also eat lots of herbs, vegetables, fruits and ancient grains. Pray and ask God to help you eat what is approved and healthy for your body.

Prayer: God, thank you for your nutritional guidance! Help me to eat what is healthy and right for my body. Teach me Lord how to eat to live and not just live to eat. Help me to build a nutritional relationship with food. Allow all that I eat to be of nourishment and sustainment for my body. God, I pray for total health and wellness all the days of my life. In Jesus Holy name I pray, Amen!

Week 31 Devotion Questions:

- Do you follow God's nutritional guide?

- Do you eat healthy foods every day?

- How do you take care of your body?

- Do you have a nutritional relationship with food?

- Do you "eat to live" and not "live to eat"?

- Do you pray for God's nourishment and sustainment?

Correlating Scripture:

- **Luke 6:44** – For every tree is known by its own fruit.

- **Romans 14:6** – He who eats, eats to the Lord, for he gives God thanks.

- **Romans 14:20** – Do not destroy the work of God for the sake of food.

- **Revelation 2:7** – "He who has an ear, let him hear what the Spirit says to the churches. To him who overcomes I will give to eat from the tree of life, which is in the midst of the Paradise of God."

Week 31 Bible Study:

- Read **Genesis 7 - 9**, **Luke 6:43-45**, **Romans 14**, and **Revelations 2:1-7**

Inspiration:

- Make your health a top priority in your life. Eat healthy foods daily.

Devotion Notes

_____

_____

_____

_____

_____

_____

_____

_____

_____

_____

_____

_____

_____

_____

Covered by God – Week 32

Genesis 7:24 - And the waters prevailed on the earth and hundred and fifty days.

God flooded the earth for 40 days and nights and then floodwaters covered the earth for 150 days. God gave earth a total restoration period of about 5 months long. God took His time and patience covering the earth so that He could restore it with His perfect rescue plan. God's timing is everything!

Sometimes in life, things may not go the way you want and then you are looking for an immediate change. Instead of wanting things rushed, take the time to seek God and ask Him to give you patience and to keep you under His covering. Before starting a new job, business, project, move, or relationship, take time to evaluate the pros and cons of your past experiences and then pray and ask God's vision for your plans. Learn to be still and stay covered under God until He says the time is right for your next move or plan.

Prayer: God, thank you for keeping me covered at all times! At times when I want immediate change, help me to be patience. When I feel the need to rush, help me to be still. Help me to see Your vision, make the best decisions, and wait on Your timing! Thank you God for being so good to me all the time! In Jesus mighty name I pray, Amen!

Week 32 Devotion Questions:

- Have you asked God for total restoration? Of spirit, heart, mind, body, soul?

- Do you believe God's rescue plan for you?

- Have you asked God of your heart's true desires?

- Do you pray before making all decisions?

Correlating Scripture:

- **Genesis 1:2** – And the Spirit of God was hovering over the face of the waters.

- **Psalm 46:10** – Be still, and know that I am God; I will be exalted among the nations, I will be exalted in the earth!

- **Psalm 84:11** – For the Lord God is a sun and shield; the Lord will give grace and glory; no good thing will He withhold from those who walk uprightly.

- **Nehemiah 9:6** – You alone are the Lord; You have made Heaven, the Heaven of Heavens, with all their host, the earth and everything on it, the seas and all that is in them, and You preserve them all. The host of Heaven worships You.

- **Colossians 1:17** – And He is before all things, and in Him all things consist.

Week 32 Bible Study:

- Read **Nehemiah 9**, **Psalm 46**, **Psalm 84**, and **Colossians 1**

Inspiration:

- Ask for God's vision for your plans.

- Learn to be still and patient. God's timing is always best!

- Pray and seek God's guidance for all matters!

Devotion Notes

_____

_____

_____

_____

_____

_____

_____

_____

_____

_____

_____

_____

_____

_____

Abundance – Week 33

Genesis 9:7 - "And as for you, be fruitful and multiply; bring forth abundantly in the earth and multiply in it."

God commands you to be fruitful, multiply, and bring forth abundantly in the earth. God wants you to repopulate and have children so family generations will continually grow. God awards a laboring man with a wife who will bear forth children from her womb for him. Children are a gift and reward from God.

God has a blessing of abundance waiting for you! He says to bring forth abundantly. This means that God has already given you the blessings, He just need you to perform your works to bring forth the abundance! Your labor will bring you abundance and prosperity; success and wealth! The man that labors will be blessed all the days of his life. The wife will be like a fruitful grapevine and flourish in her home. The children will be like olive plants that thrive and produce future generations.

Prayer: God, thank you for blessing me abundantly! Thank you for joy, health and wealth! I pray for strength and endurance to perform the works that You have created for my life! Allow my labor to bear fruit that will be a blessing unto You and others Lord! Please continually be a fence around my children and help them to thrive and succeed. Bless my family God with the fruit of Your Holy Spirit! In Jesus sovereign name I pray, Amen!

Week 33 Devotion Questions:

- In what ways does God's glory show through your labors?

- Are you bringing forth abundantly? Blessing God abundantly?

- Do you fear the Lord and walk in His ways?

Correlating Scripture:

- **Psalm 127:3** – Behold, children are a heritage from the Lord, the fruit of the womb is a reward.

- **Psalm 128:2** – When you eat the labor of your hands, you shall be happy, and it shall be well with you.

- **Ephesians 3:20** – Now to Him who is able to do exceedingly abundantly above all that we ask or think, according to the power that works in us.

Week 33 Bible Study:

- Read **Psalm 127**, **Psalm 128**, and **Ephesians 3**

Inspiration:

- Pray and ask God to allow your labor to bring forth an abundance of blessings to you and your family.

Devotion Notes

Rainbow – Week 34

Genesis 9:13 – "I set My rainbow in the cloud, and it shall be for the sign of the covenant between Me and the earth."

Genesis 9:16 - "The rainbow shall be in the cloud, and I will look on it to remember the everlasting covenant between God and every living creature of all flesh that is on the earth."

God is so awesome! God made a covenant with all creatures that He will never again destroy all life on earth. Just like this covenant, God keeps all His promises to you. Allow the rainbow to be a symbol of God's triumph; as in a banner of victory. God is victorious and will cover you always!

God is wonderful and will forever be with you! Next time you see a rainbow in the sky, look upon it and thank God for His greatness! Take the time to observe and embrace the beauty of the rainbow and allow yourself to connect spiritually with God in that moment. Allow the sight of the rainbow to fill your heart and soul with joy and reassurance that God is always covering and protecting you. Know that God is mighty and has placed His bow in the clouds just for you; how awesome is that!

Prayer: God, thank you for your everlasting covenant! Your rainbow is a gift of blessed assurance! To know that You will always cover and protect me brings me peace and comfort! Thank you Lord for your mighty victories and blessings over my life! I give all my worship and praises unto You God! You are Jehovah Nissi, my Banner! In Jesus victorious name I pray, Amen!

Week 34 Devotion Questions:

- Do you know that God's covenant is everlasting?

- Has God revealed His promises to you? What are God's promises to you?

- Do you wear God's "banner of victory"? Do you claim your victory in advance?

- Do you enjoy the beauty of the rainbow?

Correlating Scripture:

- **Psalm 20:5** – We will rejoice in your salvation, and in the name of our God we will set up our banners! May the Lord fulfill all your petitions.

- **Psalm 147:8** – Who covers the heavens with clouds, who prepares rain for the earth, who makes grass to grow on the mountains.

Week 34 Bible Study:

- Read **Genesis 9**, **Psalm 20**, and **Psalm 147**

Inspiration:

- Praise God for His greatness every time you see a rainbow!

Devotion Notes

_____

_____

_____

_____

_____

_____

_____

_____

_____

_____

_____

_____

_____

_____

_____

_____

Divided Nations – Week 35

Genesis 11:9 - Therefore its name is called Babel, because there the Lord confused the language of all the earth; and from there the Lord scattered them abroad over the face of all the earth.

After the flood, God divided the nations and scattered families to different continents of the earth. The origin of the human race began with Adam and Eve before the flood. After the flood, the human race originated from Noah's family. God later separated families and each clan identified by different languages, territories, and national identities.

The beginning of different ethnicities and cultures formed from the scatter. So, no matter where you are in the world, we all originated from the same place and are God's family! God commanded that you shall love your neighbor as yourself! Take the time to show love and kindness to everyone you encounter every day. Be a blessing by serving and loving others all over this land!

Prayer: God, thank you for all families of the earth! Allow us all to see beyond our differences and come together as one people living in one land. God, please fill the hearts of all with your unconditional and unwavering love. Let us live amongst each other and display agape love for one another at all times. God, you command that we shall love our neighbors as ourselves, help us to do so! In Jesus mighty name we pray, Amen!

Week 35 Devotion Questions:

- Do you love others as you love yourself? Treat others with respect?

- Do you disregard race, ethnicity, and gender and simply love people for who they are?

- Are you aware you are in kinship with everyone in the world through God?

Correlating Scripture:

- **Leviticus 19:18** – You shall not take vengeance, nor bear any grudge against the children of your people, but you shall love your neighbor as yourself: I am the Lord.

- **Luke 10:27** – So he answered and said, "You shall love the Lord your God with all your heart, with all your soul, with all your strength, and with all your mind, and your neighbor as yourself.

- **1Corinthians 13:13** – And now abide faith, hope, love, these three; but the greatest of these is love.

- **Galatians 3:26** – For you are all sons of God through faith in Christ Jesus.

Week 35 Bible Study:

- Read **Genesis 10-11, Leviticus 19, Luke 10:21-37, 1Corinthians 13** and **Galatians 3:26-4:7**

Inspiration:

- We are all God's children! We are brothers and sisters in Christ!

- Do something kind for a different person every day this week.

Devotion Notes

A Great Nation – Week 36

Genesis 12:2 - I will make you a great nation; I will bless you and make your name great; and you shall be a blessing.

God told Abram that in him all families of the earth shall be blessed! God has promised you blessings! Just as God told Abram, you too shall know that your name shall be great and you shall be a blessing! You have to be secure in whose you are and wear the image of God proudly! You are God's royal child and He has already blessed you before your birth! Take pride in the fact that you are God's heir, you are His and He is yours!

Your name is great and your family is great! Speak boldly and declare the blessings that God has for you and your family! Maya Angelou once said "When you learn, teach. When you get, give." God will enlarge your territory when He knows that you are a willing vessel that will teach and give unto others. Perform your works and do the Will that God has for your life!

Prayer: God, thank you for your many blessings! You have promised to always be with me and I thank you Lord! I, too, promise to love and honor your name God at all times! Thank you for my family, our health and wealth! Allow each individual to be a blessing to someone else! Put a praise upon our lips that will glorify You forever! Thank you God for your unconditional love! We give You all the glory, honor, and praise! In Jesus magnificent name I pray, Amen!

Week 36 Devotion Questions:

- Do you know God has made your name great and has promised blessings waiting for you?

- Are you confident in your identity? As God's Heir? As God's Warrior?

- Are you a willing and working vessel of God?

- Do you teach and give to others?

Correlating Scripture:

- **Acts 3:25** – You are sons of the prophets, and of the covenant which God made with our fathers, saying to Abraham, 'And in your seed all the families of the earth shall be blessed.'

- **Romans 8:17** – And if children, then heirs, heirs of God and joint heirs with Christ, if indeed we suffer with Him, that we may also be glorified together.

- **Titus 3:7** – That having been justified by His grace we should become heirs according to the hope of eternal life.

Week 36 Bible Study:

- Read **Genesis 12, Acts 3:19-26, Romans 8:1-17,** and **Titus 3**

Inspiration:

- Become a working vessel of God! Be a blessing!

Devotion Notes

Victory – Week 37

Genesis 14:16 – So he brought back all the goods, and also brought back his brother Lot and his goods, as well as the women and the people.

Genesis 14:20 - And blessed be God Most High, who has delivered your enemies into your hand. And he gave him a tithe of all.

Abram was courageous and went to protect his family and take back what was captured! God helped Abram defeat the enemies! This world is in the midst of a spiritual warfare and Satan will do anything to destroy you or take your joy away. Just like Abram, you too have to be courageous and stand firm in the midst of these warfares. You have to speak out against all evil forces and allow God to fight your battles for you! All you have to do is just activate your faith, pray, sing praises unto God and then watch the devil flee! And because you love God, all things will work together for your good!

What Satan meant for evil, God will turn it around for your good! God will always protect you, your family and your possessions that He has blessed you with. With God on your side, no one can destroy you! You are victorious and have God's glory upon you at all times! God gives you His protection and love always and forever!

Prayer: God, thank you for your glory! Thank you for fighting all battles on my behalf! I know that all things will work together for my good! God, allow Your Will for my life to be fulfilled according to Your purpose! God, you are

Holy and righteous! I bless Your name and shout all praises unto You! In Jesus victorious name I Pray, Amen!

Week 37 Devotion Questions:

- Do you have a courageous heart?

- Do you speak against and rebuke evil forces in the atmosphere?

- Have you activated your faith? Do you give God praise?

Correlating Scripture:

- **Deuteronomy 20:4** – For the Lord your God is He who goes with you, to fight for you against your enemies, to save you.

- **Psalm 20:1** – May the Lord answer you in the day of trouble; may the name of the God of Jacob defend you.

- **Romans 8:37** - Yet in all these things we are more than conquerors through Him who loved us.

- **1Corinthians 15:57** – But thanks be to God, who gives us the victory through our Lord Jesus Christ.

Week 37 Bible Study:

- Read **Genesis 13-14, Deuteronomy 20:1-4, Psalm 20, Romans 8:18-39**, and **1Corinthians 15:50-58**

Inspiration:

- Don't try to fight battles alone, let God fight all your battles! He'll give you victory!

Devotion Notes

Shield of Protection – Week 38

Genesis 15:1 – After these things the word of the Lord came to Abram in a vision, saying, "Do not be afraid, Abram. I am your shield, your exceedingly great reward."

God spoke to Abram to let him know that He is his shield of protection. You have to heed to the voice of God and know that He has you guarded against anything that is meant for evil. You have to be strong in the Lord and wear the full armor of God. **Ephesians 6:11-18** teaches you to stand firm with the belt of truth, the breastplate of righteousness, the gospel of peace, the shield of faith, the helmet of salvation, the sword of the Spirit and to pray in the Spirit always. All you have to do is just stand strong with your feet pressed and planted in Christ, and then give God your prayers and praises!

Give praise until your battles are won and then repeat the process all over again. For we are against evil forces every day, you must give God your prayers daily! Wear your praise always and then watch God triumph for you! God is your shield of protection!

Prayer: God, thank you for your shield of protection! Thank you for fighting my battles and giving me victory always! God, your protection brings me peace. I can go about my day knowing that Your covering is fenced all around me! Thank you God for keeping me safe away from all hurt, harm and dangers. I place my faith in You Lord and give all praises unto You God! In Jesus triumphant name I pray, Amen!

Week 38 Devotion Questions:

- Are you strong in the Lord? Are your feet pressed and planted in Christ?

- Do you wear the full armor of God?

- Do you read your Bible every day? Pray in the Spirit always?

Correlating Scripture:

- **Deuteronomy 33:29** – Happy are you, O Israel! Who is like you, a people saved by the Lord, the shield of your help and the sword of your majesty! Your enemies shall submit to you, and you shall tread down their high places.

- **2Samuel 22:3** – The Lord is my rock and my fortress and my deliverer; the God of my strength, in whom I will trust; my shield and the horn of my salvation, my stronghold and my refuge; my Savior, You save me from violence.

- **Psalm 3:3** - But You, O Lord, are a shield for me, my glory, and the One who lifts up my head.

- **Psalm 28:7** – The Lord is my strength and my shield; my heart trusted in Him, and I am helped; therefore my heart greatly rejoices, and with my song I will praise Him.

Week 38 Bible Study:

- Read **Genesis 15-16, Deuteronomy 33, 2Samuel 22, Psalm 3, Psalm 28**, and **Ephesians 6:10-20**

Inspiration:

- Read your Bible daily! Wear the full armor of God and pray in the Spirit always!

Devotion Notes

_____

_____

_____

_____

_____

_____

_____

_____

_____

_____

_____

_____

_____

_____

_____

_____

Almighty God – Week 39

Genesis 17:1 – When Abram was ninety-nine years old, the Lord appeared to Abram and said to him, "I am Almighty God; walk before Me and be blameless.

God appears to Abram and tells that He is El-Shaddai, God Almighty! God then commands Abram to serve Him faithfully and live a blameless life! Know that God is a Sovereign God who has all mighty powers and blessings over you. Love God with your whole heart and serve Him faithfully! When you give God your all, He in return gives you unlimited blessings and sufficiency! God's provision will sustain you, nourish you and protect you always.

God has an everlasting covenant with you and promises to make you extremely fruitful. God will give you adequate resources to do the works that will fulfill the purpose He has for your life! God will provide for all of your needs. Give your all to the Almighty God; for what you do for Christ will last! Get ready to see your blessings blossom and flourish!

Prayer: God, thank you for your almighty powers! Thank you for your everlasting covenant with me! Give me the strength to do the works that will fulfill your purpose for my life! Allow all that I do to reflect God's glory! I thank you for your abundance of blessings! God, you provide for all of my needs and I am forever grateful! I give all glory, honor and praise unto you Lord for you are the Almighty God! In Jesus powerful name I pray, Amen!

Week 39 Devotion Questions:

- Do you serve God faithfully? Live a blameless life?

- Do you give God your all? Your heart, your works, your everything?

- Can you testify of God's blessings?

Correlating Scripture:

- **Psalm 89:8** – O Lord God of hosts, who is like You, O Lord? Your faithfulness also surrounds You.

- **Psalm 91:1** – He who dwells in the secret place of the Most High shall abide under the shadow of the Almighty.

Week 39 Bible Study:

- Read **Genesis 17-21**, **Psalm 89**, and **Psalm 91**

Inspiration:

- Be accountable and responsible for all your actions. Live righteously!

Devotion Notes

_____

_____

_____

_____

_____

_____

_____

_____

_____

_____

_____

_____

_____

_____

_____

My Provider – Week 40

Genesis 22: 14 - And Abraham called the name of that place, The-Lord-Will-Provide, as it is said to this day, "In the Mount of the Lord it shall be provided."

Jehovah Jireh is your provider! God blesses you according to your trust and obedience in Him. When you obey God's voice, He then provides you with all that you need in life! Put your trust in God and He will not forsake you! Your trust and obedience to God will bring His provision over you!

God will continually multiply your blessings and give you prosperity when you are obedient to Him! Keep your faith in God, do your works of God, praise boldly unto God, and pray to God always! Do these things and He will keep His promises and provisions unto you! God is omnipotent and has the power to provide for all of your needs!

Prayer: God, thank you for providing for me! Life brings about many trials and through all my trials, you have protected and provided for me! Lord, I thank you for your sustaining and nourishing me! You provide me the strength and endurance I need to everyday to do Your Will! You provide me the comfort and encouragement I need to never give up on my tasks! I thank you for your mighty powers and provisions! I give all thanks unto You Lord! In Jesus Holy name I pray, Amen!

Week 40 Devotion Questions:

- Are you obedient to God? Complete your godly tasks?

- Do you thank God for His provision?

- Do you praise God boldly?

Correlating Scripture:

- **Psalm 23:1** – The Lord is my shepherd; I shall not want

- **Psalm 65:9** – You visit the earth and water it, you greatly enrich it; the river of God is full of water; you provide their grain, for so You have prepared it.

- **Ezekiel 34:15** – "I will feed My flock, and I will make them lie down," says the Lord God.

- **2Corinthians 9:8** – And God is able to make all grace abound toward you, that you, always having all sufficiency in all things, may have an abundance for every good work.

Week 40 Bible Study:

- Read **Genesis 22, Psalm 23, Psalm 65, Ezekiel 34**, and **2Corinthians 9:6-15**

Inspiration:

- Be generous in your giving for God loves a cheerful giver.

Devotion Notes

_____

_____

_____

_____

_____

_____

_____

_____

_____

_____

_____

_____

_____

_____

Praise and Worship – Week 41

Genesis 24:48 - And I bowed down my head and worshipped the Lord, and blessed the Lord God of my master Abraham, who had led me in the way of truth.

Abraham's servant is on his journey to find Isaac a wife. As he is on his mission, he faithfully prays to God and ask for God to help him succeed. He prays within his heart, worships and praises God as He leads him on the right path. The servant trusts that God's love and faithfulness will direct him correctly. You, also have to follow the example of Abraham's servant. When faced with troubles, trials, and complexities, just sincerely pray within your heart and ask God to help you succeed on your journey. As you pray and speak to God, He is already making a way for you. Offer unto the Lord the praises of your mouth! Bless God with your worship!

God's love and faithfulness will bear forth the fruits of your labor. Just keep working hard and you will achieve your goals. God is the lamp upon your feet and will direct your pathway. **Psalm 20:4-5** says "May he give you the desire of your heart and make all your plans succeed. We will shout for joy when you are victorious and will lift up our banners in the name of God. May the Lord grant all your requests." God is your banner, your Jehovah Nissi who will answer your prayer and honor your praise and worship!

Prayer: God, thank you for hearing my heart! Thank you for answering my prayers! Thank you for making a way for me and directing me on the right path to succeed. I have faith in You and know that I will see the fruits of my labor.

May you bless me with the desires of my heart as I offer my praise and worship unto you Lord! Thank you for your blessings of overflow in advance! God, I come to you on this day believing and claiming my prosperity and know that it is already granted! In Jesus faithful name I pray, Amen!

Week 41 Devotion Questions:

- Do you ask God to lead you the right way?

- Do you believe and obey God's Holy Word?

- Ask God to keep you on a righteous path.

- Do you trust God to direct your pathway?

- Do you bless God with your worship?

- Do you believe God has already granted you prosperity?

Correlating Scripture:

- **Psalm 150:6** – Let everything that has breath praise the Lord. Praise the Lord!

- **Matthew 6:6** – But you, when you pray, go into your room, and when you have shut your door, pray to your Father who is in the secret place; and your Father who sees in secret will reward you openly.

- **John 4:24** – God is Spirit, and those who worship Him must worship in spirit and truth.

Week 41 Bible Study:

- Read **Genesis 23-24, Psalm 20, Psalm 150, Matthew 6** and **John 4**

Inspiration:

- Pray to God with a sincere heart! Worship and praise His Holy name!

Devotion Notes

_____

_____

_____

_____

_____

_____

_____

_____

_____

_____

_____

_____

_____

_____

A Blessed Life – Week 42

Genesis 25:8 - Then Abraham breathed his last and died in a good old age, an old man, and full of years, and was gathered to his people.

Genesis 6:3 - And the Lord said, My spirit shall not strive with man forever, for he is indeed flesh; yet his days shall be one hundred and twenty years.

Abraham lived to be of an old man with a life full of blessed years. God has declared that our flesh shall be no more than 120 years old. May God grant you a blessed life full of many joyous years. May God give you great health and prosperity all the days of your living! I pray that you will make your nutrition a top priority so that you may fulfill God's declaration of your existence! **Leviticus 11** tells of all the clean nutritional foods that are to be eaten. As we eat to live and not live to eat, we too can live to be of a good old age.

Ephesians 6:2 says "Honor your father and mother," which is the first commandment with promise: "that it may be well with you and you may live long on the earth." God has made the promise that if you honor your parents, your days will be long on earth. May God grant you a blessed life!

Prayer: God, thank you for the gift of life! I pray that I will live a long and fulfilling life! Upon my final breath, I ask that Heaven be my eternal home! Allow me to join my ancestors and rejoice unto You Lord! For our bodies are flesh and will go back to dust. Grant my Spirit to rise and have everlasting life in Heaven! I pray to become one of your angels and watch over my loved ones from above.

May my Spirit always live within the souls of those I love. Grant my loved ones to see my face and hear my voice in their dreams when my life on earth is over. Keep my love for them in their hearts always God. I'm thanking you in advance for a blessed life with an abundance of love, joy, peace, happiness, healthiness and prosperity! In Jesus prosperous name I pray, Amen!

Week 42 Devotion Questions:

- Is God blessing your life with joyous days?

- Are you placing nutrition as top priority in your life?

- Do you value your health and wellness?

- Do you honor your mother and father? Your guardians and elders?

Correlating Scripture:

- **Deuteronomy 4:40** - You shall therefore keep His statues and His commandments which I command you today, that it may go well with you and with your children after you, and that you may prolong your days in the land which the Lord your God is giving you for all time.

- **Deuteronomy 6:4-5** – "Hear, O Israel: The Lord our God, the Lord is one! You shall love the Lord your God with all your heart, with all your soul, and with all your strength.

- **Job 10:12** – You have granted me life and favor, and Your care has preserved my spirit.

- **Job 33:4** – The Spirit of God has made me, and the breath of the Almighty gives me life.

Week 42 Bible Study:
- Read **Genesis 25, Deuteronomy 4, Deuteronomy 6:1-9, Job 10, Job 33**, and **Ephesians 6:1-4**

Inspiration:
- Worship God only and honor your parents so that you may have a long blessed life on earth!

Devotion Notes

Foreign Place – Week 43

Genesis 26:3 - Dwell in this land, and I will be with you and bless you; for to you and your descendants I give all these lands, and I will perform the oath which I swore to Abraham your father.

Genesis 26:13 - The man began to prosper, and continued prospering until he became very prosperous.

God told Isaac to dwell in the foreign land for he would be blessed. Sometimes in life, we too are placed in foreign places or unfamiliar situations. During these temporary states, we must believe and trust God for his help. Isaac dwelled in the land and later received an abundance of blessings just as God promised him. God also wants to bless you exceedingly. Our foreign states of life are only temporary and won't last long. God will move on your behalf as you wait for His promises to be fulfilled.

God will strengthen you to help you move out of that unfamiliar place. God promised that He will always be with you. To receive the abundance of blessings that God has oath to you, you need to keep your faith in God, obey God, read His Holy Word, and increase your prayer life. By doing these things, you will receive the royal benefits God has specifically for you!

Psalm 23:6 says "Surely goodness and mercy shall follow me all the days of my life: and I will dwell in the house of the Lord forever." When in your foreign place, just dwell there and know that God's goodness, mercy, love, blessings and prosperity is about to overflow in your life!

Prayer: God, thank you for the foreign place! During my most uncomfortable moments, I will stay put and trust you to move on my behalf! For it is in the foreign land where my blessings will continually flow. You prepare the table before me and cause my cup to run over! God, I thank you for my overflow of blessings! I give all praise, glory and honor unto You God! In Jesus royal name I pray, Amen!

Week 43 Devotion Questions:
- Have you ever been in a "foreign place", a place of trials and unfamiliarity?

- Have you prayed for God's strength to move out that uncomfortable foreign place?

- Do you see God's glory and royal riches working in your life?

Correlating Scripture:
- **Psalm 5:12** – For You, O Lord, will bless the righteous; with favor You will surround him as with a shield.

- **Psalm 9:9** – The Lord also will be a refuge for the oppressed, a refuge in times of trouble.

- **Psalm 25:4-5** – Show me Your ways, O Lord; teach me Your paths. Lead me in Your truth and teach me, for You are the God of my salvation; on You I wait all the day.

- **Isaiah 41:10** - Fear not, for I am with you; be not dismayed, for I am your God. I will strengthen you, yes, I will help you, I will uphold you with My righteous right hand.

- **John 14:2-3** - "In My Father's house are many mansions; if it were not so, I would have told you. I go to prepare a place for you. And if I go and prepare a place for you, I will come again and receive you to Myself; that where I am, there you may be also.

Week 43 Bible Study:
- Read **Genesis 26, Psalm 5, Psalm 23, Isaiah 41**, and **John 14**

Inspiration:
- Praise God in the foreign place for He will move you to a place of prosperity!

Devotion Notes

Reflected Image – Week 44

Genesis 26:28 – "We have certainly seen that the Lord is with you."

Genesis 26:29 – "You are now the blessed of the Lord."

King Abimelech could plainly see that the Lord was with Isaac. God's image should also reflect greatly off of you so that others can clearly see that the Lord is with you. Treat people well and keep peace between yourself and others. Show love and kindness to everyone everywhere. By doing so, God's favor will pour upon you! God will bless you immensely when you do His works. God has promised blessings for your obedience. If you walk in the ways of God, the Lord will grant you abundant prosperity. God will bless all the work of your hands and make you the head. As a child of God, you are entitled to His glorious riches! Walk in God's image and He will forever have unlimited resources to supply all of your needs!

Prayer: God, thank you for your reflected image in me! May the grace of God forever be within my Spirit so that others know that you are with me everywhere I go. Assist me O God to confess to others the greatness of Your name! Allow your light O God to shine within me so that others may see your good deeds. I will rejoice and be glad for I know that my greatest reward of all is in Heaven! Thank you for your abundant prosperity Lord! I will wear Your image proudly forever and always! In Jesus sovereign name I pray, Amen!

Week 44 Devotion Questions:

- Is God embedded in your spirit? Do you carry the Holy Spirit everywhere you go?

- Do others see that God is with you always?

- How do you confess the greatness of God to others?

- Are you proud to wear God's image forever and always?

Correlating Scripture:

- **1Corinthians 15:49** – And as we have borne the image of the man of dust, we shall also bear the image of the heavenly Man.

- **2Corinthians 3:18** – But we all, with unveiled face, beholding as in a mirror the glory of the Lord, are being transformed into the same image from glory to glory, just as by the Spirit of the Lord.

Week 44 Bible Study:

- Read **Genesis 26-27, 1Corinthians 15:35-49**, and **2Corinthians 7-18**

Inspiration:

- Let others see God's glory, love, and power through you!

Devotion Notes

_____

_____

_____

_____

_____

_____

_____

_____

_____

_____

_____

_____

_____

_____

_____

God's Tenth – Week 45

Genesis 28:22 – "And this stone which I have set as a pillar shall be God's house, and of all that You give me I will surely give a tenth to You."

God provides for you always! God watches over you daily and protects you on your journey. God gives you shelter to house you, food to eat and clothes to wear. God grants you an abundance of peace and blessings! God is always providing and making a way for you! Every day, take time to worship and praise God for all that He has done for you! Let Him know you are grateful and give thanks unto Him! God has already given you plenty and will yet still continue to overflow you with numerous blessings! Vow to give God a tenth of your blessings as a way to say Thank You Lord!

Prayer: God, thank you for supplying all my needs! Thank you for giving me the desires of my heart! Thank you for granting me peace, joy, love, and happiness! I vow to honor you with my praise and worship! I vow to honor you by giving a tenth of my blessings back to you Lord! Thank you for your glory and riches! Your name is worthy of all of my praise! In Jesus glorious name I pray, Amen!

Week 45 Devotion Questions:
- Are you thankful God supply all your needs?

- Do you give a tenth of your blessings back to God?

- Do you give to others in need, your church or community?

- Do you honor God? Are you grateful? Do you thank God for His blessings?

Correlating Scripture:
- **Deuteronomy 28:6** – "Blessed shall you be when you come in, and blessed shall you be when you go out."

- **Deuteronomy 28:8** – "The Lord will command the blessing on you in your storehouses and in all to which you set your hand, and He will bless you in the land which the Lord your God is giving you."

- **Proverbs 3:9** - Honor the Lord with your possessions, and with the first fruits of all your increase.

- **Ephesians 3:20-21** – Now to Him who is able to do exceedingly abundantly above all that we ask or think, according to the power that works in us, to Him be glory in the church by Christ Jesus to all generations, forever and ever. Amen.

- **Philippians 4:19-20** – And my God shall supply all your need according to His riches in glory by Christ Jesus. Now to our God and Father be glory forever and ever. Amen."

Week 45 Bible Study:
- Read **Genesis 28-32, Deuteronomy 28:1-14, Proverbs 3,** and **Philippians 4**

Inspiration:
- Honor God with your possessions and witness Him bless you exceedingly and abundantly in all that you do!

Devotion Notes

Friendly Smile – Week 46

Genesis 33:10 – "I have seen your face as though I had seen the face of God, and you were pleased with me."

Because you are God's own image, seeing your friendly face is like seeing the face of God! God has graced you in His sight that others who encounter you can also experience the smile of God! Find favor in the Lord and be kind to others. In **Matthew 22:39**, God commands "you shall love your neighbor as yourself." Be gracious and pleasing to people you meet. God has called us to just simply love. Open your heart, and express love and kindness all the time! God's love should reflect through your friendly smile and be used for His glory!

Prayer: God, thank you for my friendly smile! Thank you for creating me with a uniqueness that displays your glory! Thank you for your unconditional love! God, you love and find favor in me! I am forever thankful and grateful to reflect your image Lord! Thank you for all the many blessings you have given to me! I praise you in advance and thank you for my heart's desires! I put my complete faith and trust in You! There is none like You! I love you God! In Jesus magnificent name I pray, Amen!

Week 46 Devotion Questions:

- Do you present friendly smiles to others?

- Does your smile represent the face of God?

- Do others experience God through you? Do you display God's glory?

- Are you pleasing and loving to others?

Correlating Scripture:

- **Numbers 6:24-25** – "The Lord bless you and keep you; the Lord make His face shine upon you, and be gracious to you."

- **Proverbs 18:24** – A man who has friends must himself be friendly, but there is a friend who sticks closer than a brother.

Week 46 Bible Study:

- Read **Genesis 33-34, Numbers 6:22-27, Matthew 22:34-40,** and **Proverbs 18**

Inspiration:

- Your smile should reveal God's grace and favor!

Devotion Notes

One True God – Week 47

Genesis 35:3 – And I will make an altar there to God, who answered me in the day of my distress and has been with me in the way which I have gone.

Genesis 35:11 – Also God said to him: "I am God Almighty, be fruitful and multiply; a nation and a company of nations shall proceed from you, and kings shall come from your body."

Jacob advised his household to remove all pagan idols and to purify themselves. There is only one true God who is in Heaven and reigns above all. Trust in God for He is your help and shield. God will be with you during all your pains, sufferings, dangers and troubles. With the Lord on your side, you will prevail all! God will guide and lead you on a righteous and victorious path! God is with you wherever you go. Pray to God for He hears your voice and listens to your prayers. Give God all the glory for His unconditional love and faithfulness! Offer unto God a mighty praise and bless His Holy name! May God richly bless your soul and give you continual increase forever more!

Prayer: God, thank you for your sovereignty! You are God the Father, God the Son and God the Holy Spirit! Thank you for placing your divine Spirit and power within me Lord! Thank you God for your help and shield! I could not go through the trials of life without you! You guide my path and lead me to my destiny! You are my provider and protector! You keep my family and I away from unseen dangers and fight invisible battles on our behalf! God, I will forever bless, honor, and glorify your Holy name always! In Jesus Sovereign name I pray, Amen!

Week 47 Devotion Questions:

- Do you believe God Almighty is the one true God?

- Do you love God with all your heart, soul, and mind?

- Do you initiate prayer and worship God with a pure and clean heart?

Correlating Scripture:

- **Deuteronomy 4:35** – To you it is was shown, that you might know that the Lord Himself is God; there is none other besides Him.

- **Deuteronomy 6:4** – "Hear, O Israel: The Lord our God, the Lord is One!

- **Isaiah 45:14** – "Surely God is in you, and there is no other God."

- **1John 5:7** – For there are three that bear witness in Heaven: the Father, the Son, and the Holy Spirit; and these three are one.

- **1John 5:20** – And we know that the Son of God has come and has given us an understanding, that we may know Him who is true; and we are in Him who is true, in His Son Jesus Christ. This is the true God and eternal life.

Week 47 Bible Study:
- Read **Genesis 35-44, Deuteronomy 4-6, Isaiah 45:14-25,** and **1John 5**

Inspiration:
- Love God with all your heart, mind, soul and strength!

Devotion Notes

_____

_____

_____

_____

_____

_____

_____

_____

_____

_____

_____

_____

_____

_____

_____

Preparations – Week 48

Genesis 45:7 - And God sent me before you to preserve a posterity for you in the earth, and to save your lives by a great deliverance.

Just like God preserved life in advance for Joseph and his brothers, He also has preservations for you too! God walks ahead of you on your journey and defeats all unknown battles that were to come your way! God will lead the way for your successes if you just trust and believe in Him! Follow His lead and trust His preparations! The Lord intercedes and intervenes on your behalf breaking chains of trials and tribulations so that you may prosper! Only God has the power to go before you and move mountains solely just for you!

Let God direct and guide you toward your destiny! As God prepares the way for your blessings, keep your faith, increase your prayer life with Him, and do the works He has called you to do! God's glory, riches, prosperity and blessings are waiting ahead for You!

Prayer: God, thank you for your preparations! You have gone before me to prepare the way for my deliverance! God, I thank you in advance for all blessings that are coming my way! You provide all my needs and I am grateful Lord! You are my Sovereign God who break chains and move mountains just for me! I place all my trust in You God! In Jesus glorious name I pray, Amen!

Week 48 Devotion Questions:

- Are you thankful that God walks ahead of you on your journey?

- Do you wait on the Lord? Do you trust God?

- Have you increased your prayer life with God?

Correlating Scripture:

- **Deuteronomy 1:30-31** – The Lord your God, who goes before you, He will fight for you, according to all He did for you in Egypt before your eyes, and in the wilderness where you saw how the Lord your God carried you, as a man carries his son, in all the way that you went until you came to this place.

- **Psalm 40:2** – He also brought me up out of a horrible pit, out of the miry clay, and set my feet upon a rock, and established my steps.

- **Isaiah 45: 2-3** – "I will go before you and make the crooked places straight; I will break in pieces the gates of bronze and cut the bars of iron. I will give you the treasures of darkness and hidden riches of secret places, that you may know that I, the Lord, who call you by your name, Am the God of Israel."

Week 48 Bible Study:

- Read **Genesis 45, Deuteronomy 1:19-33, Psalm 40,** and **Isaiah 45:1-13**

Inspiration:

- Let God prepare the way for you and establish your steps!

Devotion Notes

_____

_____

_____

_____

_____

_____

_____

_____

_____

_____

_____

_____

_____

_____

_____

_____

_____

God's Best – Week 49

Genesis 45:18 – Bring your father and your households and come to me; I will give you the best of the land of Egypt, and you will eat the fat of the land.

Genesis 45:20 - Also do not be concerned about your goods, for the best of all the land of Egypt is yours.

God will give you His best for your praise! Acknowledge the Lord at all times and carry His Spirit in your soul always! Don't worry about stuff, for God has waiting blessings for you to enjoy! For your praise and prayers, God will replace your trauma with triumph and your sorrow with solace! God wants an intimate relationship with you! The Lord is longing for a passionate prayer warrior that will declare and announce His greatness! Allow your soul to receive the ultimate experience of God! Keep your hope and faith in the Lord! Rejoice in the blessings that God has for you; His best!

Prayer: God, thank you for your greatness! You are excellent and mighty in all thy ways! Thank you God for your best! Thank you for being the keeper of my mind, heart, body, soul and spirit! I will shout praises unto your Holy name, for you are great! You are Holy! You are righteous! You are mighty! You are victorious! I give all glory, honor and praise unto You Lord! I give you my best in exchange for your best! In Jesus worthy name I pray, Amen!

Week 49 Devotion Questions:

- Do you present God with your best everything (praise, worship, works)?

- Do you carry God's Spirit in your soul always?

- Do you have an intimate relationship with God?

- Are you a passionate prayer warrior?

- Do you declare and announce God's greatness? Shout praises to Him?

- Do you fully "experience" God and rejoice in His love?

Correlating Scripture:

- **Deuteronomy 26:11** – So you shall rejoice in every good thing which the Lord your God has given to you and your house.

- **Deuteronomy 26:18** – "Also today the Lord has proclaimed you to be His special people, just as He promised you, that you should keep all His commandments, and that He will set you high above all nations which He has made, in praise, in name, and in honor, and that you may be a holy people to the Lord your God, just as He has spoken."

- **Psalm 21:6** – For You have made him most blessed forever; You have made Him exceedingly glad with your presence.

- **2Corinthians 9:8** – And God is able to make all grace abound toward you, that you, always having all sufficiency in all things, may have an abundance for every good work.

- **2Corinthians 9:15** – Thanks be to God for His indescribable gift!

Week 49 Bible Study:
- Read **Genesis 45-48**, **Deuteronomy 26**, and **2Corinthians 9**

Inspiration:
- Make God exceedingly glad with your presence!

- Put God first in your life and He will give you His best!

Devotion Notes

Highly Blessed – Week 50

Genesis 49:25-26 - By the God of your father who will help you, and by the Almighty who will bless you with Blessings of Heaven above, Blessings of the breasts and of the womb. The Blessings of your father have excelled the Blessings of my ancestors, up to the utmost bound of the everlasting hills.

You are highly blessed by God! God has special blessings that are unique and specific just for you! Use your talents and gifts to glorify God. Dedicate your life to the Lord for He will open doors for you that no man can close! Pour your heart out to God and He will pour His divine favor upon you!

Trust God wholeheartedly for your life is in His hands! When you acknowledge God's sovereignty, a serene peace will fall on your soul and dwell in your spirit! It's peaceful and reassuring to know that God is in control of everything and has your back at all times! Absorb God's unconditional and everlasting love as He pours continuous blessings upon you!

Prayer: God, thank you for your divine favor upon my life! I devote myself to you! I will use my talents to bless and serve You Lord! Thank you for your love, joy and peace! Thank you for your everlasting love and care! I'm grateful for all blessings that you bestow upon me God! I'm thankful for your many blessings! I give praises to you now and in advance for what I have and for what's yet to come! All glory belongs to You! In Jesus sovereign name I pray, Amen!

Week 50 Devotion Questions:

- Are you aware that you're highly blessed by God?

- Do you know that God's blessings are everlasting?

- Do you bless God with your special talents and gifts?

- Have you dedicated your life to God?

Correlating Scripture:

- **Deuteronomy 2:7** – For the Lord your God has blessed you in all the work of your hand. He knows your trudging through this great wilderness. These forty years the Lord your God has been with you; you have lacked nothing.

- **Deuteronomy 28:1-2** – "Now it shall come to pass, if you diligently obey the voice of God, to observe carefully all His commandments which I command you today, that the Lord your God will set you high above all nations of the earth. And all these blessings shall come upon you and overtake you, because you obey the voice of the Lord your God."

- **Psalm 139:14** – I will praise You, for I am fearfully and wonderfully made, marvelous are Your works, and that my soul knows very well.

- **Proverbs 8:32** – "Now therefore, listen to me, my children, for blessed are those who keep my ways."

- **Ephesians 1:3** – Blessed be the God and Father of our Lord Jesus Christ, who has blessed us with every spiritual blessing in the heavenly places in Christ.

- **1Peter 2:9** – But you are a chosen generation, a royal priesthood, a holy nation, His own special people, that you may proclaim the praises of Him who called you out of darkness into His marvelous light; who once were not a people but are now the people of God, who had not obtained mercy but now have obtained mercy.

Week 50 Bible Study:
- Read **Genesis 49, Deuteronomy 2:1-9, Deuteronomy 28:1-14, Psalm 139, Proverbs 8, Ephesians 1**, and **1Peter 2**

Inspiration:
- You are highly favored and blessed by God!

Devotion Notes

_____

_____

_____

_____

_____

_____

_____

_____

_____

_____

_____

_____

_____

_____

_____

Forgive & Reconcile – Week 51

Genesis 50:17 – 'Thus you shall say to Joseph: "I beg you, please forgive the trespass of your brothers and their sin; for they did evil to you." Now, please, forgive the trespass of the servants of the God of your father."

When you are offended by others, pray and ask God to release your resentment or anger. Don't ever hold bitterness in your heart. Let go of the pain, give your problems to God and let Him replace your hurt with happiness! Forgive that person and their faults and make amends. Relationships are purposeful and God places each person in your life for a reason. Communicate, remove the tensions, and resolve the problem.

Reconcile to restore a healthy and happy relationship with others. When you reconcile, you display a spirit of meekness. When you forgive, you demonstrate God's love and peace. In **John 13:34**, God commands "that ye love one another; as I have loved you." You are to forgive, reconcile, and display God's agape love to one another. Your relationship with God should reflect your relationship with others! The Lord forgave you, so you must also forgive others. All things work together for good to those who love the Lord and do accordingly to His Will!

Prayer: God, thank you for your grace and mercy! You forgave me of my sins and I thank you! Help me to forgive and love others even when I have been wronged. Help me to ask for forgiveness if I've hurt anyone. Help me seek the Will of God to reflect your love and kindness unto others. Release all hurt and pain for total peace and happiness!

Thank you for restoring my life with healthy relationships and meaningful bonds that display your unconditional love! God, let your peace and love dwell within my heart! In Jesus loving name I pray, Amen!

Week 51 Devotion Questions:

- Do you treat others well? Keep peace between you and others? Avoid hostility?

- Do you forgive others when they offend or hurt you?

- Do you give your troubles to God?

- Do you ask for forgiveness if you've hurt anyone?

- Do you reconcile after a quarrel or disagreement?

- Does your relationship with God reflect your relationship with others?

Correlating Scripture:

- **Matthew 6:14** - For if you forgive men their trespasses, your heavenly Father will also forgive you.

- **Colossians 3:13** – Bearing with one another, and forgiving one another, if anyone has a complaint against another; even as Christ forgave you, so you also must do."

- **2Corinthians 2:7-8** – You ought rather to forgive and comfort him, lest perhaps such a one be swallowed up with too much sorrow. Therefore I urge you to reaffirm your love to him.

- **James 3:18** – Now the fruit of righteousness is sown in peace by those who make peace.

- **1John 4:7** – Beloved, let us love one another, for love is of God; and everyone who loves is born of God and knows God.

Week 51 Bible Study:
- Read **Genesis 50, Matthew 6, Colossians 3, 2Corinthians 2:3-11, James 3**, and **1John 4 – 5**

Inspiration:
- Let go of grudges, forgive, and settle all disagreements.
- Don't let stubbornness cause you to miss out on your blessings!

Devotion Notes

_____

_____

_____

_____

_____

_____

_____

_____

_____

_____

_____

_____

_____

_____

_____

Meant for Good – Week 52

Genesis 50:20 - But as for you, you meant evil against me; but God meant it for good, in order to bring it about as it is this day, to save much people alive.

With God, you are standing against all unseen evil forces! Satan's evil intentions to harm and destroy you are defeated by God! God has already turned every bad intention around for your good! The battle is already won so walk proudly and confidently in your everlasting victory! Thank God for His protection and glorify Him! Give God your praise and triumph every time! In this world, you will have tribulation. However, just like Joseph, your blessings will overflow amongst your hardships! For every trial, trouble, or suffering you endure; give God a greater praise and witness your deliverance! Worship His Holy name for God is great!

Allow God to lead your every thought, spoken word, and deed! Stand firm in the Lord and have peace in God! Keep your faith and wear the full armor of God always! Worry about nothing and pray about everything! When you pray in the Spirit your soul remains free in Christ! God is always for you; therefore no one can ever stand against you! You inherit God's victory, riches and glory! Nothing in this world can ever separate you from God's triumph or His love for you!

Prayer: God, thank you for your endless victory! You defeat my enemies and give me your glory! Thank you for turning the bad around for my good! I thank you God for keeping me forever in your care! You brought me through many trials! I will always give your Holy name the highest praise! You are Holy, Just, Sovereign, Righteous, Mighty, Victorious, Magnificent, Wonderful, Amazing, and Loving! In Jesus Great name I pray, Amen!

Week 52 Devotion Questions:

- Do you love God and are of good cheer?

- Do you walk proudly in your everlasting victory?

- Do you allow God to lead your every thought, spoken word, and deed?

- Do you have peace in God? Is your soul free in Christ?

Correlating Scripture:

- **Deuteronomy 20:4** – 'For the Lord your God is He who goes with you, to fight for you against your enemies, to save you.'

- **John 16:33** – "These things I have spoken to you, that in Me you may have peace. In the world you will have tribulation; but be of good cheer, I have overcome the world."

- **Romans 8:28** - And we know that all things work together for good to those who love God, to those who are the called according to his purpose."

- **Romans 8:31** – What then shall we say to these things? If God is for us, who can be against us?

- **Psalm 115:14-15** – May the Lord give you increase more and more. You and your children. May you be blessed by the Lord, who made Heaven and earth.

Week 52 Bible Study:
- Read **Deuteronomy 20**, **John 16**, **Romans 8**, and **Psalm 114**

Inspiration:
- Give thanks to God and serve Him in sincerity and in truth! Lift your soul to the Lord and all that you do, do in the name of Jesus Christ!

Devotion Notes

_____

_____

_____

_____

_____

_____

_____

_____

_____

_____

_____

_____

_____

_____

_____

ABOUT THE AUTHOR

Ministry has always been a part of Angela's life! She accepted Christ as a pre-teen and was baptized at her home church. As a young girl, she sang on the youth choir. Her father and mother both encouraged her to sing God's praises! Singing Gospel Music has always been her passion and connection to God! She loves to praise and worship God's Holy Name!

At 14 years old, her Grandmother Sadie gifted her with her first personal Holy Bible. She was taught and inspired to read the Word of God. Grandmother Sadie particularly made sure that Angela stayed in prayer by remembering the Lord's Prayer (**Matthew 6:9-13**) and was comforted by learning **Psalm 23**.

God placed a calling on Angela's life to write inspirational messages for Him! Her Grandmother Sadie visited her in a dream and confirmed that it was time for her to write a devotional for God! Without delay, she began to write until its completion! Angela thanks God for His love and endurance! All messages and prayers in Bread of Heaven was given to her through God's Holy Spirit!

Angela accepted God's call to minister to His people! She is a Minister and Sunday School Curriculum Writer. Angela loves writing and teaching Bible lessons to children, teens, and adults. She encourages all to depend on and trust God always. Her mission is for others to learn how to apply God's Word in all aspects of their life every day.

Angela is also the co-owner of **Wade Christian Publishing LLC,** where authors are assisted with professional editing, layout, design, and publishing services. She thanks God for all that He has done and continues to do in her life to benefit the well-being of others!

Angela is also the author of **Bread of Heaven Devotional Prayer Journal** and the Children's Book, **Kamdyn's Adventures**.

Angela holds an M.B.A. and a B.S. She is married to Colonel Dwayne Wade and they are the parents of Donovan and David. She is the daughter of Deacon David and Deaconess Cheryl Williams, and of Deacon Danny and Minister Marilyn Wade. Angela loves to read, write, sing, cook, teach, travel, and enjoy outdoor activities.

I pray you've been blessed in your devotionals! May God's Holy Spirit continually feed your soul and guide you daily! May God be the lamp upon your feet and the light upon your path! I'm praying that God reveals His divine purpose for your life! Proudly do the works that God has designed for you to do! Place God first in everything that you do, and as a reward, God will bless you with His serene peace, unconditional love, everlasting joy, illuminating glory, and an abundance of His blessings & prosperity!

God's Favor,
Minister Angela Wade

Wade Christian Publishing

EPHESIANS 2:10

www.wadepublishers.com

info@wadepublishers.com